THE
POWER
of a
PROMISE

RALPH L. RINGER

Pacific Press®
Publishing Association
Nampa, Idaho | www.pacificpress.com

Cover design by Steve Lanto
Cover design resources from iStockphoto.com | francescoch
Inside design by Aaron Troia

The author assumes full responsibility for the accuracy of all facts and quotations as cited in this book.

Additional copies of this book may be purchased by calling toll-free 1-800-765-6955 or by visiting AdventistBookCenter.com.

Unless otherwise noted, all Scripture quotations are taken from the New King James Version®. Copyright © 1982 by Thomas Nelson. Used by permission. All rights reserved.

Scripture quotations marked KJV are from the King James Version.

Library of Congress Cataloging-in-Publication Data

Names: Ringer, Ralph L., 1945- author.
Title: The power of a promise / Ralph L Ringer.
Description: Nampa : Pacific Press Publishing Association, 2019.
Identifiers: LCCN 2018060309 | ISBN 9780816364725 (pbk. : alk. paper)
Subjects: LCSH: Covenants—Biblical teaching. | Covenants—Religious
    aspects—Christianity. | Theology, Doctrinal.
Classification: LCC BS680.C67 R56 2019 | DDC 231.7/6—dc23 LC record
    available at https://lccn.loc.gov/2018060309

December 2018

Contents

What's a Covenant?

How many covenants have you entered into so far in your life? If your response is something like, *Covenants?* you're not alone. We don't use this word much anymore, but nevertheless, we make covenants all the time. Student loans, car leases, and home mortgages are covenants. So are marriage licenses, wills, and business contracts. Even clicking the "I agree" box when downloading an app is a covenant.

In the biblical context, *covenant* is an old word that has important meanings for understanding and building a personal relationship with God. A new understanding of covenants starts with the history of this old-fashioned word. *Covenant* finds its origins in four languages—Hebrew, Greek, Latin, and Old French.[1] *Covenant* simply means a "mutual compact to do or not do something, a contract," such as vows between a married couple or an agreement between a borrower and a lender. The word also means a "contract, promise, pledge, solemn resolve, vow, testament, promise of legal validity," such as student loan agreements, car leases, home mortgages, and marriage licenses. *Covenant* can also describe a personal relationship with God as a type of legal commitment: "the promises of God as revealed in the Scriptures conditioned on certain terms on the part of humanity."[2] Although it is a spiritual commitment, the covenant of baptism can also be legally important, since in some instances a baptismal certificate can be legally admissible in the place of a birth certificate.

A covenant, such as marriage, is a two-sided promise; it is a commitment between two persons, not just a commitment to God. But more importantly, covenants are about God's commitment to us. This book highlights God's side of the covenant as the "everlasting covenant," or God's unchanging commitment to us.

God's everlasting covenant is the story of His love, faithfulness, and commitment to saving fallen humanity. Woven from the many covenants throughout Scripture, God's one everlasting covenant forges a perfect, beautiful, lasting bond between the eternal God and us, His children. When we sign our ordinary covenants, such as home mortgages and marriage licenses, or click the "I agree" boxes on apps, we believe that we will benefit from doing so, and we believe that the other party will keep his or her side of the promise. Sometimes it can be hard to see the benefits or to believe the promise of God's everlasting covenant; it seems almost too good to be true. But God wants us to believe what is hard for us to believe. *Covenant?*

Believers of all backgrounds can become God's remnant. Tracing covenant-keeping—from Adam and Eve to Noah, from Abraham to Moses, from Daniel to Paul, from Paul to John the revelator—this book offers a new angle on covenants as strategies for dealing with an imperfect world and on the remnant, whether Jew or Gentile, whose covenant-keeping is centered on the Messiah's coming and sacrifice. The goal of this book is to help readers understand how their individual covenant-keeping experiences are interwoven with God's everlasting covenant, now and for eternity.

---

1. *Online Etymology Dictionary*, s.v. "covenant," accessed October 22, 2018, https://www.etymonline.com/word/covenant.

2. *Webster's Third New International Dictionary, Unabridged*, s.v. "covenant," accessed October 22, 2018, http://unabridged.merriam-webster.com.

Acknowledgments

I would like to thank my daughter, Dr. Laurie Ringer, English professor at Burman University, for encouraging me to write this book. She also coached me in both the writing and editing of my book before I sent it to the publisher.

I would like to thank Jeff Zaremsky, director of *Shalom Adventure* web magazine, for helping me to understand Jewish history better. This gave me a deeper understanding of the Scripture included in this book.

I would like to thank Dr. Alexander Bolotnikov, director of the Shalom Center, for sharing his deep insights about the Hebrew Scripture, which has helped me to be more scripturally accurate.

I would like also to thank my wife, Nancy, for her support, encouragement, and understanding while I was writing my book.

CHAPTER 1

Adam and Eve: Covenants to Deal With an Imperfect World

*C*ovenants? What's the deal with covenants? Covenant-keeping is complicated. In our world today, people don't always keep their covenants, or promises. Loans go into default, marriages end in divorce, contracts get broken. Yet every day, people honor contracts, keep promises, and safeguard marriages. Covenants are supposed to make life better in our confusing world, but it can be hard to know who and what to believe in.

Given all the complexities and uncertainties, it can help to understand why and how covenants came about. Our imperfect world does not represent God's perfect ideal, so covenants are necessary strategies for helping us deal with an imperfect world. The covenants God makes with us shape our lives for the better—now and for eternity. As we understand the history of covenants in Scripture and the need for them, we will see how God's covenants with us give us hope. Let's look at Genesis to see why and how covenants started.

At first, God's creation was perfect; there was no need for covenants as strategies for dealing with imperfection. In His perfect world, God and humans lived the relationship of the everlasting covenant. The *Andrews Study Bible* describes creation as something like a potter forming vessels from clay.[1] Coming close to earth, God created a people with whom He could have a loving relationship. "This people have I formed for Myself; they shall declare My praise" (Isaiah 43:21). These people would bond with Him and be a people with whom He would live out the perfection of the everlasting covenant.

Intimately close to Adam, "the LORD God formed man of the dust of the ground, and breathed into his nostrils the breath of life; and man became a living being" (Genesis 2:7). God took the same loving care in creating Eve as He did when He created Adam. "The LORD God said, 'It is not good that man should be alone' " (verse 18). A deep sleep came upon Adam, and God removed one of his ribs and created Eve from it. The rib (verses 21, 22), in proximity to Adam's vital organs, including his heart, could symbolize marital love and a special emotional bond for the two of them as partners in a lifelong covenant relationship. "So husbands ought to love their own wives as their own bodies; he who loves his wife loves himself" (Ephesians 5:28). In the love Adam and Eve had for each other, they would see God's love for them. They were the crowning act in God's perfect creation of this world.

Adam and Eve, together with God, are the basis of the relationship involved in the everlasting covenant. Just as God entered into a loving, everlasting covenant relationship with them, they were to enter into a similar covenant relationship with their surroundings. God blessed them and sent them forth to be fruitful and multiply (Genesis 1:28). God commissioned Adam and Eve to care for all life in the Garden of Eden (Genesis 2:15). They were not to tend the Garden as landscapers; they were to commune closely with God's creation, naming each animal and honoring the covenant to care for the earth (Revelation 11:18). We can only imagine what Adam and Eve must have felt about life in the Garden. Perhaps they were filled with joy and happiness as they saw God's love reflected in the playful animals. Perhaps they realized His delight in variety as they named the beautiful flowers and fruit-filled plants with their infinite colors, shapes, smells, and sizes.

Their first full day together in the Garden marked their marriage as holy. God completed His Creation work by resting on the seventh day. "Then God blessed the seventh day and sanctified it, because in it He rested from all His work which God had created and made" (Genesis 2:3). By sanctifying the seventh day, God set apart the Sabbath (Exodus 20:8–11) for a holy purpose as a sign of the covenant between Himself and His people, testifying that He is the Lord who sanctifies and makes us holy (Ezekiel 20:12, 20).

God's rest on the seventh day didn't just mark the end of His work or the beginning of the marriage covenant between Adam and Eve; it was a weekly reminder of their relationship with God and with the perfect world that He created. This is the beginning of the everlasting covenant; God says,

> "For your Maker is your husband,
> The Lord of hosts is His name;
> And your Redeemer is the Holy One of Israel;
> He is called the God of the whole earth"
> (Isaiah 54:5).

The Sabbath is like a wedding band; it symbolizes a spiritual marriage between us and our Creator. It is a weekly reminder honoring the spiritual wedding of God to His people. He has promised us that keeping His Sabbath holy proclaims that we are in a covenantal marriage with Him.

God planted the tree of life (Genesis 2:9; 3:22) in the Garden

10

to make His covenant with Adam and Eve everlasting—so that they could enjoy life for eternity. This tree was a reminder that God wanted there to be no end to His covenant with them. However, this perfect world did not last.

Adam and Eve found out the hard way that when it comes to making and keeping covenants, it can be difficult to know whom and what to believe. In the perfect world of the Garden of Eden, they had no frame of reference by which to deal with imperfections such as deception, discomfort, or death. In love, God made a perfect world with perfect people. He intended for it to be full of joy and love for eternity. Unfortunately, Adam and Eve were not successful in dealing with the serpent's deception, and they unwittingly broke their covenant with God. Let's look at Genesis 3:1–5 and see just how they were unprepared to deal with deception.

Covenants? What does a talking snake have to do with covenants? At this point in the Genesis narrative, Adam has just named the animals (Genesis 2:20) and God has just placed the first pair in charge of "every living thing that moves on the earth" (Genesis 1:28). So far, the only ones talking have been God, Adam, and Eve. In addition, they have experienced nothing but truth in their perfect covenant with God; they are totally unprepared for untruth.

Then Satan entered the Garden in deep disguise. Just as false prophets put on "sheep's clothing" (Matthew 7:15) to deceive, Satan took on snake's clothing to sabotage Adam and Eve's covenant with God and to steal their dominion of the earth (Genesis 1:28). Satan appeared in the tree of knowledge of good and evil (Genesis 2:17; 3:3)—not in his natural form, but as an animal, specifically a serpent (Revelation 12:7–9), the most "cunning" of all the animals (Genesis 3:1). In the perfect Garden, a serpent was not a threat to its human caretakers. They could not see

11

the danger, because Satan *looked* like a serpent. They had seen serpents, but they had never seen deception.

When the smartest animal in the Garden began talking to her, Eve listened, vulnerable to curiosity and deception. A talking serpent was surprising enough to spark curiosity. *Why is it talking? What does it have to say?* After all, it was one of the animals in her care. She should not ignore it, should she? Appearing to misunderstand God's instructions, the serpent made a stealth attack. "Has God indeed said, 'You shall not eat of every tree of the garden'?" (Genesis 3:1). To Eve, this question might appear to be an honest one, but it stealthily cast doubt on God's instructions regarding the tree (Genesis 2:17) by suggesting that God had placed *all* the trees in the Garden off limits. This seed of doubt opened the possibility of questioning the covenant.

Eve straightened out the serpent's misunderstanding by clarifying that God's instruction applied only to the tree of knowledge of good and evil and that they were free to eat fruit from all the other trees (Genesis 3:2, 3). She also explained the penalty for not following God's instructions—she and Adam would "surely die" (Genesis 2:17) if they ate from the forbidden tree.

The serpent expanded the tiny doubt he had created by openly challenging God's statement. "You will not surely die" (Genesis 3:4), he declared. Just as his serpent body curling around the tree, Satan's words coiled around God's statement, reversing it and ensnaring Eve. "For God knows that in the day you eat of it your eyes will be opened, and you will be like God, knowing good and evil" (verse 5). Eve lacked a frame of reference by which to deal with this deceptive half-truth. Satan continued the insinuating lie by suggesting that God's covenant could not be broken. Basically he said, "Don't worry. You won't die. God's covenant means that you are to live eternally no matter what you do!"

Eve knew only good; she did not yet know what evil was because God's covenant with her and Adam contained only goodness and perfection. Satan introduced imperfection and deception masquerading as a missing piece of knowledge.

In spite of God's warnings, Eve's conversation with the serpent changed the way she saw the tree. Now she saw the tree as good for food, as pleasant to the eye, and as desirable for wisdom. Conned into thinking that she was missing some essential knowledge that the tree could provide and deceived into believing that this essential knowledge would not break God's covenant, Eve took the fruit. She ate it and shared the fruit with Adam, who also ate it (verse 6).

With every contract or covenant we enter into, there are consequences if it is broken. So it was also with Adam and Eve. They were deceived into breaking their covenant with God, and thus, they were shut off from its benefits. By breaking the covenant, they left themselves devoid of God's covering, leaving them naked and afraid (verses 7, 10). They hid from God and blamed each other; they even blamed God (verses 8–13). Adam (man) was cursed; the earth now had thorns and thistles, causing him to have to work hard for his bread (verses 17–19). The woman was cursed with difficult child bearing (verse 16), and the serpent was cursed to crawl on its belly (verse 14). Adam and Eve were driven out of the Garden and banished from the tree of life; they had to live with the hard lessons of doubt, deception, and death.

However, God was not willing to give up on His covenant. He immediately came to the rescue of Adam and Eve. God gave them the promise of a Messiah, saying to Satan,

> "I will put enmity
> Between you and the woman,
> And between your seed and her Seed;

He shall bruise your head,
And you shall bruise His heel"
(verse 15).

Satan would bruise Jesus' heel by having Him crucified, but Jesus would bruise, and even crush, Satan's head by totally defeating him (Romans 16:20; 1 Corinthians 15:22; Galatians 3:16).

Not only did God continue His side of the covenant with Adam and Eve by promising that one day Eve's Seed would crush the serpent's head, He provided a substitutionary atonement for them right then. God instructed Adam and Eve to sacrifice an animal to die in their place, and then He clothed them with that animal's skin (Genesis 2:21). To people who had never seen death, this sacrifice graphically illustrated Jesus' death for us as the Lamb of God (John 1:29), who clothes us with His own righteousness (Romans 10:19).

Covenants? What's the deal with covenants? Covenants are necessary because imperfection marred God's perfect creation. Adam and Eve fell for a con job in the Garden where there were only two competing voices. Today, our confusing world is full of competing voices, and it can be hard to know who and what to believe in. It's easy to look back and judge Eve and Adam, but as we deal with the difficulties involved in knowing who and what to believe in, it is helpful to understand how covenants came about and to let this understanding remind us of the serpent's modus operandi. His deception and sabotage in the Garden remind us that, like Eve, we can be deceived into breaking our covenant with God.

---

1. *Andrews Study Bible* (Berrien Springs, MI: Andrews University Press, 2010), Genesis Study Notes, s.v. "2:7 *formed.*"

CHAPTER 2

God's Everlasting Covenant: Noah Through Abraham

T he story of the 1,500[1] or so years after Adam and Eve's fall could cause us to question the purpose of covenants, so it's important to think about Noah's world as the reverse of the Garden of Eden. Eve was deceived by the serpent because she knew only perfection and goodness. But by the time God told Noah to start preaching about a coming flood, the world was so ruined by imperfection and evil that it was hard to believe in good. The world was so evil that people thought Noah's message was a con, though it was the truth. Not accepting the covenant that Noah offered cost the descendants of Adam and Eve dearly: their inability to believe Noah cost them their lives. Just as Eve couldn't imagine the serpent's evil deception, the people in Noah's day couldn't imagine a world without deception and exploitation, a world in which someone offered truth and goodness. Because of their inability to believe that Noah was not conning them but actually preaching God's covenant, all inhabitants of the earth—with the exception of eight people—were lost in the Flood! Our world today is a lot like Noah's world (Matthew 24:37–39); it can be hard to know who to believe in, and sometimes not believing in covenants can be dangerous. That's why it's so important to understand the biblical significance of God's covenants with His people.

After the Flood, God didn't have to reaffirm the everlasting covenant with Noah and his descendants—but He did. He knew it would be natural for people to wonder whether the same thing might happen in the future—whether another flood might destroy all life on earth. He also knew that covenants can be confusing to people. So God said to Noah, "Behold, I establish My covenant with you and with your descendants after you. . . . I establish My covenant with you: . . . never again shall there be a flood to destroy the earth" (Genesis 9:9, 11). By twice using the word *covenant*, God emphasized His continuing commitment to the descendants of Adam and Eve, specifically, and to Noah's family lines. Just like God's covenant with Adam and Eve, Noah's individual, local covenant arose from his unique circumstances and relationship with God, weaving him and his descendants into the everlasting covenant. God reaffirmed with Noah His commitment to salvation and His desire for a relationship with His people, which is the everlasting covenant.

Following the Flood, God's part in His covenant with Noah and his descendants was a pledge never again to destroy the world by a flood; Noah's part and that of his descendants was to believe God and to rebuild, repopulate, and maintain the post-Flood world, relying on God's grace and power.

God took this relationship so seriously that He gave us a perpetual sign of His covenant: "I set My rainbow in the cloud, and it shall be for the sign of the covenant between Me and the earth" (verse 13). The rainbow that God sets in the sky temporarily connects heaven and earth, visually and symbolically. Visually, the rainbow rests on the earth while extending into the clouds of heaven. In heaven, a rainbow surrounds

God's throne (Revelation 4:3). He surrounds Himself with His covenant promise to Noah and to us, symbolically giving Noah and his family a glimpse of heaven. Through the symbol of the rainbow, God binds Himself to us with such love that He has surrounded Himself with His covenant promise to us. In Genesis 9:16, the rainbow is referred to as the symbol of "the everlasting covenant." God wants to have an eternal loving relationship with the survivors of the Flood and all their descendants. Every time there is a rainbow, it echoes God's everlasting covenant.

About five hundred years after Noah's time,[2] Abraham (then known as Abram) entered into an individual, local covenant with God based on his unique circumstances and relationship with God. In Genesis 17, the word *covenant* is used thirteen times during God's conversation with Abraham. Nine of those times, God refers to "My covenant," showing His investment in the agreement with Abraham. Five times, God includes all "your descendants" in the covenant, also promising, "You shall be a father of many nations" (verse 4) and stating that as a result of Abraham's obedience, "all the nations of the earth shall be blessed" (Genesis 22:18). Three times, God refers to the "everlasting covenant." Abraham's covenant weaves not only his descendants but also many nations into the everlasting covenant. Through Abraham, God reaffirms His commitment to salvation and His desire for a relationship with all people—which is the essence of the everlasting covenant.

But Abraham almost breaks the covenant because God's timing is different than what Abraham imagines it should be. Abraham has lived some seventy-five years, first in his hometown of Ur and later in Haran (Genesis 11:31; 12:4). As an older man, he left his country and family home to make a new life and claim new blessings. "Now the LORD had said to Abram:

'Get out of your country,
From your family
And from your father's house,
To a land that I will show you.
I will make you a great nation;
I will bless you
And make your name great;
And you shall be a blessing' "
(Genesis 12:1, 2).

To bless future generations, Abram must uproot himself from his familial home.

Almost a quarter century later, when Abram was ninety-nine years old, God reaffirmed their covenant by changing the name Abram had had for almost a century. It was not enough to move him away from his father's country; he was to have a new name (Genesis 17:5) and a new son. God told him, "I will make My covenant between Me and you, and will multiply you exceedingly" (verse 2).

In Abraham's eyes, God appeared to have left the childbearing part of their covenant to occur a bit late. For God's covenant to work, it required that Abraham have a son to honor his father's name, to bless other nations, and to carry on his part of the covenant that God reaffirmed with Abraham.

Like Eve and like the people in Noah's day, Abraham didn't deal well with the complexities of the covenant. God had said that Abraham's own son would be his heir, and Abraham believed Him. However, Sarah (Sarai), his wife, was getting old, well past childbearing years, and she, too, was impatient for the covenant to be fulfilled. "So Sarai said to Abram, 'See now, the Lord has restrained me from bearing children. Please, go in to my maid; perhaps I shall obtain children by her.' And Abram heeded the voice of Sarai" (Genesis 16:2).

Abraham's acceptance of God's promise was a supreme act of faith, but his willingness to enter into a polygamous relationship, common in that age but nevertheless a sin, reflected his incapacity to understand the covenant that God had made with him more than a quarter century earlier (Genesis 12).

Abraham conceived a son with Sarah's servant Hagar, who became proud and "her mistress became despised in her eyes" (Genesis 16:4). The once harmonious relationship was shattered with jealousy and bitterness. Abraham still did not understand God's covenant, so when he was ninety-nine years old, the LORD reminded him of the promise. "As for Me, behold, My covenant is with you, and thou shall be a father of many nations" (Genesis 17:4). Then He clarified the covenant promise of an heir: "As for Sarai your wife, you shall not call her name Sarai, but Sarah shall be her name. And I will bless her and also give you a son by her; then I will bless her, and she shall be a mother of nations; kings of peoples shall be from her" (verses 15 and 16).

Abraham's failure to wait on God was highlighted by one of the greatest Jewish scholars who learned from Gamaliel (Acts 5:34), Saul of Tarsus, who became the apostle Paul. "If Abraham was justified by works, he has something to boast about, but not before God. For what does the Scripture say? 'Abraham believed God, and it was accounted to him for righteousness' " (Romans 4:2, 3). Abraham was so focused on bringing forth the covenant promise that he forgot that it depended on God's long-term relationship with his bloodline, starting with Isaac, the son of his wife. Moreover, the promise of salvation is God's side of the covenant to fulfill, not Abraham's.

Dealing with covenants can be challenging, and like Eve and the people in Noah's day, Abraham almost failed. Only by God's mercy did their agreement bind. Eve was deceived by the serpent, the people of Noah's day deceived themselves, and Abraham was influenced by both the sinful world he had lived in for more than a hundred years and his own misunderstanding of God's covenant.

In the next chapter, we will explore the promise and message of the Messiah's salvation through sacrifice and symbol.

1. Kenneth D. Boa, "Visual Survey of the Bible," *Holy Bible*, New King James Version (Nashville, TN: Nelson, 1990), 1088, 1089.

2. Boa, "Visual Survey," 1088, 1089.

CHAPTER 3

Moses and the Covenant With Israel

About five hundred years after Abraham, Moses' mother wove a basket of bulrushes to cradle her son, a tiny ark she hoped would float him to a safer and better life (Exodus 2:1–4). The bulrush basket is a useful way of thinking about the covenant in Moses' generation. After some four hundred years of slavery (Exodus 12:40, 41), people needed material reminders of God's presence in dark times when it could be hard to remember the promises made to Abraham so long ago.

Together, the bulrush basket, the stone tablets of the Decalogue, the wilderness tabernacle, and the ark of the covenant formed a space where Immanuel cradled Israel in their journey to the Promised Land. This chapter explores these material reminders of the covenant that were woven into the experience of Moses' generation.

As God had promised in His covenant, Abraham's descendants did multiply—through Abraham's son Isaac and his grandson Jacob. Jacob's name was eventually changed to Israel (Genesis 32:28), so his descendants became known as "the children of Israel," or later, simply, "Israel." During Jacob's time, there was a famine, and he and his family went to Egypt to survive. There, they multiplied and grew strong as God had promised—so much so that Pharaoh became afraid of them (Exodus 1:2–14).

He enslaved the Israelites; but slavery did not stop their rapid growth. So Pharaoh commanded that all the baby boys born to the Israelites should be killed (verses 15–22). It was during this time that Moses was born.

Moses's parents disobeyed Pharaoh's command to throw all of Israel's baby boys into the river (verse 22). They hid him three months and then made an ark of bulrushes to float him to safety on the river (Exodus 2:2, 3). Moses's sister Miriam watched from a distance (verse 4) as Pharaoh's daughter found Moses in the little ark and had compassion on the Hebrew infant.

The little woven basket preserved Moses' life in a time of crisis for him and his parents. It was a safe space that made it possible for God's plan for his life to be fulfilled. In the same way, God's everlasting covenant surrounded His people, Israel, even in their Egyptian bondage, preserving their lives and making it possible for God's plan for their salvation—both temporal and spiritual—to be fulfilled.

Miriam asked Pharaoh's daughter whether she wanted her to get a nurse for the baby from the Hebrew women. In this way, Moses' own mother was able to raise him in his early years before Pharaoh's daughter took him to become her son. Moses grew to adulthood in Pharaoh's palace.

Moses lived a life of luxury in the palace, but he knew his people were slaves and that their lives were very hard. When he was about forty years old, he saw an Egyptian beating a Hebrew, and in a fit of rage, Moses killed the Egyptian taskmaster (verses 11, 12). His outrage may be understandable, but Moses had an anger-management problem. Later, he struck the rock in anger instead of speaking to it as directed by God (Numbers 20:8–13), and he broke the first stone tablets containing the Ten Commandments when he saw Israel worshiping the golden calf (Exodus 32:19). In all these instances, Moses failed to wait on

God to deal with the problem and instead let his anger control his actions.

Pharaoh heard about Moses murdering the Egyptian task-master and "sought to kill Moses" (Exodus 2:15). Moses fled for his life to the land of Midian, where he became a shepherd for forty years (verses 15–22). It now seemed that Moses was helpless to do anything to help Israel and that God had forgotten Israel; however, God had not forgotten Moses, Israel, or His covenant. When Israel cried out to God, He "remembered His covenant with Abraham, with Isaac, and with Jacob" (verse 24). Sometimes we mess up as Moses did, running ahead of God and taking things into our own hands when it seems that God has forgotten. However, God has not forgotten His covenant or us.

Moses spent four decades living the life of a shepherd before God spoke to him from a burning bush (Exodus 3:1–4). "Come now, therefore," God told Moses, "and I will send you to Pharaoh that you may bring My people, the children of Israel, out of Egypt" (verse 10). To Moses, it seemed impossible to go back to Egypt, where he was a wanted man. He began to make excuses. At eighty years old (Exodus 7:7), he had pretty much forgotten the Egyptian language from lack of use for forty years. He didn't feel up to the task.

In response, God assured him, "I will certainly be with you. And this shall be a sign to you that I have sent you: When you have brought the people out of Egypt, you shall serve God on this mountain" (Exodus 3:12). The mountain where Moses was now herding sheep would be the place where God would talk to him, where he would receive the Ten Commandments and receive the instructions about the tabernacle.

Moses doubted that the Israelites would believe that God had sent him. In reply, God gave him miraculous signs to perform in order to convince them (Exodus 4:2–4, 6, 7). Moses claimed he was not eloquent and was slow of speech. God replied, "I will be with your mouth and teach you what you shall say" (verse 12). He also pointed out that Aaron, Moses' brother, could serve as his spokesman (verses 14–16).

So Moses reluctantly returned to Egypt. But when Moses and Aaron requested that Pharaoh let Israel go, the Egyptian ruler refused (Exodus 5:4; 7:14). God sent ten plagues on the Egyptians as Pharaoh continued to refuse (Exodus 7:14–11:10). The tenth plague brought death to all the first-born males in every family that did not have the blood of the Passover lamb on the doorframe of their home. The Passover was a symbol of Israel's covenant with God that offered new revelations regarding their relationship with God. As a result of the plagues, especially the death of the firstborn, which disrupted all the power lineage of Egypt, Pharaoh drove Israel out of Egypt (Exodus 11:1; 12:39).

The Lord led Israel with a pillar of cloud by day to shade the people on their way. He led them with a pillar of fire by night so that they could see their way and not stumble or fall (Exodus 13:21, 22). It wasn't long, however, before Pharaoh changed his mind yet again and pursued Israel with all his army. The Israelites were very afraid (Exodus 14:10) when they saw the Egyptians coming after them. The Red Sea was in front of them, and the Egyptians were coming at them from behind. It seemed there was no way out. Exodus 14:13 says, "Moses said to the people, 'Do not be afraid. Stand still, and see the salvation of the Lord, which He will accomplish for you today. For the Egyptians whom you see today, you shall see again no more forever.' " Moses assured Israel that God was going to save them and fight for them. The Angel of God and the pillar of fire that was leading Israel moved behind them, between them and the Egyptians (verses 19, 20). The pillar of fire was light to Israel but darkness to the Egyptians—like a wall all night to keep them from attacking Israel.

God divided the waters of the Red Sea with a strong east wind and dried the sea bottom for Israel to walk through (verses 21, 22). The Egyptians pursued Israel into the sea, and God brought the waters over the Egyptians and drowned all of them (verses 22–28). Israel saw what the Lord did and believed Him and Moses.

God also gave the Israelites manna to eat for the forty years they were in the wilderness (Exodus 16:35), which showed His care for His covenant people. Yet even with their lengthy experience of God's care, Moses and Israel struggled to fully understand and embrace the covenant, so God wove material reminders into their daily lives. He provided water and food in the wilderness. He kept their clothes from wearing out (Deuteronomy 8:4). He kept them from sickness and shielded them from their enemies.

Their experience as slaves in Egypt left its mark on the Israelites and on Moses. It made it difficult for them to trust, and it caused them to have anger-management problems. Their trust issues manifested themselves over and over in their murmuring against God when things did not go well, and they easily turned their anger on Moses. Moses himself found it easy to become angry at the people and even with God. Anger, when it is out of control, is destructive. God patiently worked with His people and with Moses, giving them tools to deal with and manage their anger and lack of trust. These material reminders were designed to help them remember how God had loved and led them in the past and to enable them to deal with their anger. The tablets of the Decalogue, the tabernacle with its symbolism and services, and the ark of the covenant, representing God's presence and His covenant with them—all these were tools to help them trust Him and fully embrace the everlasting covenant.

Good anger-management tools help individuals try to put their lives on a more positive track in four ways: (1) cognitive reconstruction (changing our way of thinking), (2) problem solving, (3) changing our environment, and (4) better communication. We will see how the tools God gave Israel helped them deal with their anger.

The basket of bulrushes

The basket, or ark, that Moses' mother wove from bulrushes and covered with pitch was a material reminder to the people of how the various covenants are woven together into God's everlasting covenant to save the lives of His covenant people. The tiny ark saved Moses and was a visual reminder of how God saves the lives of His covenant people through His everlasting covenant.

Like the rushes woven together to make the bulrush basket, God's covenant wove its way through the daily lives of the Israelites in Moses' time, surrounding them like a kind of ark to carry them through the challenges of life during and after the Egyptian captivity. Moses' parents were doubtless angry at the injustice of Pharaoh's decree to kill all the Israelite male babies. But they channeled that anger into a positive response and found a way to save Moses with a basket of bulrushes. Likewise, the Israelites could find peace by choosing to wrap themselves in the protection and freedom of God's everlasting covenant rather than continue to feed on their anger over their years of Egyptian bondage.

The tablets of the Decalogue

Three months after Israel left Egypt, they came to the wilderness of Sinai and camped before Mount Sinai (Exodus 19:1, 2). Moses went up to God on the mountain (verse 3). There, God told Moses to tell Israel, "Now therefore, if you will indeed obey My voice and keep My covenant, then you shall be a special treasure to Me above all people. . . . And you shall be to Me a kingdom of priests and a holy nation" (verses 5, 6). Israel's response is found in verse 8: "All that the LORD has spoken we will do." Then the Israelites sanctified themselves (verses 9–15).

When God gave the Ten Commandments to Moses and Israel, He reminded them, "I am the LORD your God, who brought you out of the land of Egypt, out of the house of bondage" (Exodus 20:2). God had just brought His people out of Egypt and slavery. In their new freedom, He gave them the Ten Commandments, which the book of James calls "the perfect law of liberty" (James 1:25; 2:10–12). In their slavery, the Israelites did not have a good understanding of God and did not know how to obey Him.

God spoke and wrote the Ten Commandments as a basis on which to understand the covenant and our relationship with Him and our fellow human beings. Love is the foundation of the Decalogue. Jesus said, "If you love Me, keep My commandments" (John 14:15). Love should be our motive for obedience. In the new covenant that God gives us, He helps us keep His commandments by writing them in our minds and hearts. "For this is the covenant that I will make with the house of Israel after those days, says the LORD: I will put My laws in their mind and write them on their hearts; and I will be their God, and they shall be My people" (Hebrews 8:10). God wants to have a loving covenant relationship with His people. When He writes His laws, the Ten Commandments, in our hearts and minds, we will want to be in harmony with Him and His commandments.

The tablets of the Decalogue were a crucial element in helping Israel deal with its anger issues. As slaves, they had been subject to the commands of their masters. They had to obey whether they wanted to or not. They were angry and depressed at the way they were treated. But being God's servants was different. God ruled them in love. He did not give them His commandments to force them into obedience against their will. He offered them His commandments as a path of freedom—freedom from sin and hatred and anger. As they allowed Him to write His commandments in their minds and hearts, as they internalized the law of liberty and obeyed from the motive of love, their anger would fade away and they would enjoy the blessings of the everlasting covenant.

In Exodus 24:7, 8, Moses confirmed the covenant between God and Israel. "Then he took the Book of the Covenant and read in the hearing of the people. And they said, 'All that the LORD has said we will do, and be obedient.' And Moses took the blood, sprinkled it on the people, and said, 'This is the blood of the covenant which the LORD has made with you according to all these words.' "

After the covenant was ratified, God called Moses to come up the mountain. "Then the LORD said to Moses, 'Come up to Me on the mountain and be there; and I will give you tablets of stone, and the law and commandments which I have written, that you may teach them' " (verse 12). The Ten Commandments were written in stone to show that they were a permanent and an unchangeable part of God's covenant.

The wilderness tabernacle

"Moses was on the mountain forty days and forty nights" (verse 18). On the mountain, not only did God give Moses the two tablets of stone upon which the Ten Commandments were written but He also spoke to Moses all that is recorded in Exodus chapters 25 through 31 and much of the rest of the book through chapter 40. In addition, twenty of the twenty-seven chapters in Leviticus start with the words, "The LORD spoke to Moses." In these chapters, God goes into detail of why and how to build the wilderness tabernacle and its furnishings, how to make the priest's clothes, how to conduct the daily and weekly services, the yearly feasts, and more. What an exciting and informative time this must have been for Moses. This ongoing conversation with God helped Moses and Israel with their anger management by restructuring their view of Him and changing their environment.

God and Israel ratified the covenant, and now God wanted to dwell with His people. That's why He said, "Let them make Me a sanctuary, that I may dwell among them" (Exodus 25:8). From the very beginning, God wanted to be close to His people. In fact, He made them in His own image (Genesis 1:26) so that they could relate to Him better. After Adam and Eve sinned, they were facing death (Genesis 2:17). However, God was not willing to give up on His covenant people, and He immediately came to the rescue of this first pair in the Garden. God promised them a Messiah, saying,

> "I will put enmity
> between you and the woman,
> and between your seed and her Seed;
> He shall bruise your head,
> and you shall bruise His heel"
> (Genesis 3:15).

That promise, of a coming Messiah who would gain the victory over Satan, gave Adam and Eve hope that their relationship with God could be restored. The Messianic promise of Isaiah 7:14 uses the name *Immanuel* and is quoted in Matthew 1:23, where it is applied to Jesus, "God with us." The sanctuary and its services and sacrifices illustrated the life, work, and ministry of the Messiah (Psalm 77:13). Scripture points to the sanctuary as revealing what God would do to fulfill His covenant with His people. Psalm 77:13 says, "Your way, O God, is in the sanctuary." God has revealed His covenant and His plan for salvation through the symbolism of the sanctuary, its furniture, and its services.

The sanctuary is also called the tabernacle in Scripture. Its importance in Scripture is indicated by the fact that *sanctuary* occurs 155 times, and *tabernacle* appears 296 times.[1] The word *tabernacle* can refer to a house, a dwelling-place, the human body, or a portable tent.[2] God wanted a home on earth where He could dwell with His covenant people. God gave Moses instructions about how He wanted the sanctuary/tabernacle and its furnishings to be built (Exodus 25:9). The tabernacle was made portable so that it could be moved and always be with God's covenant people.

Israel had spent 430 years in Egypt, about 400 of those years as slaves. They had seen the temples of the gods of Egypt, but they had no place to worship their God. Now, the tabernacle would be a place where God could dwell among them and they could come and worship Him on a daily basis. It was a physical presence among them, making real to them the fact that God was always present in their midst. It was a place they could go to find forgiveness for their sins through the sacrifices carried out there. The solemn ceremonies and feasts reinforced their sense of being God's chosen people. All these things helped them deal with the stress and pressures of their wilderness wanderings. The tabernacle was a significant aid in helping them manage their anger and stress.

A cloud covered the tabernacle by day and fire by night, and all Israel could see it (Exodus 40:38). In addition, the glory of

God filled the tabernacle (verse 34). When the cloud was lifted up and moved, Israel followed it. When it settled down, they camped (verses 36–38). The presence of the tabernacle was a material reminder of God's presence, and the cloud and fire were continual evidence of His dwelling with them. This helped to change their thinking about God, who wanted to be with them on a daily basis, help them, solve their problems, and protect them.

The sanctuary/tabernacle, its furniture, and its services were all symbolic of the life and ministry of the Messiah. The courtyard represents the Messiah, accessible in the midst of His covenant people; here they could come to meet with Him (Hebrews 9).

In the courtyard surrounding the tabernacle was the altar of burnt offering, which symbolized the Messiah's sacrificial death for our sins. This is where all the sacrifices were offered. Anyone could come and witness the morning and evening sacrifice or any other offering. The courtyard is where they brought their sin offerings, which would take away their sin and guilt. The bronze laver, which symbolized how the Messiah washes away sin, was also in the courtyard.

The tabernacle had two rooms—the Holy Place and the Most Holy Place. The Holy Place was where the priests performed all the daily and yearly services in the tabernacle, except those taking place on the Day of Atonement. The Day of Atonement was the only service that occurred in the Most Holy Place. Only the high priest could enter the Most Holy Place, and he could do so only once each year.

The Holy Place contained three pieces of furniture, each symbolizing the Messiah and His work. The table of shewbread represented the Messiah as the Bread of Life that sustains us and gives us eternal life (John 6:35, 41, 51). The golden lampstand symbolized the Messiah as the Light of the world that brings light and eternal life in this dark world to all who believe in Him (Isaiah 9:2; Luke 1:79; John 8:12; 9:5; 12:46). The altar of incense symbolized the Messiah as a sweet-smelling aroma to take away the stench of sin (Ephesians 5:2; Psalm 141:2; Revelation 5:8; 8:3, 4). Israelites knew the priests were ministering for them each day in the Holy Place, and this helped them feel they were in a caring environment instead of the harsh slavery they had known in Egypt.

The ark of the covenant

The ark of the covenant was an earthly symbol, a material reminder of God's heavenly throne, but it was more than just a symbol. Just as the tabernacle was the place where God could "dwell among" His people (Exodus 25:8), the ark of the covenant was God's earthly throne—the seat of God's glory from which shone the cloud by day and fire by night that covered the tabernacle (Exodus 40:34–38). The cloud and fire were evidence of God's presence on His earthly throne—evidence that the Israelites could feel they were in a safe environment and that God cared for them and would help them deal with their problems on a daily basis.

The Most Holy Place in the tabernacle was where the high priest did his work each year on the Day of Atonement. The ark of the covenant was the only piece of furniture in the Most Holy Place. Inside the ark were the Ten Commandments, symbolizing God's justice; on top of the ark was the mercy seat where the high priest sprinkled the blood of the sacrifice on the Day of Atonement, symbolizing forgiveness and God's mercy. Above the mercy seat shone the brightness of God's presence (Leviticus 16:2), surrounded by the wings of two cherubim. Unlike the annual work of the earthly high priest, the Messiah's self-sacrifice occurred once when He "appeared to put away sin by the sacrifice of Himself" (Hebrews 9:26; see also verses 22–28). Through His self-sacrifice, the Messiah embodied the mercy that was symbolized by the mercy seat; all the other sacrifices represent the Messiah's sacrifice that takes away sin. The Messiah, like the tabernacle, is also God "with us" (Matthew 1:23).

When God gave Moses His instructions regarding the construction of the tabernacle, it had been about twenty-five hundred years since He had given the promise of the Messiah to Adam and Eve. Israel had been in slavery for about four hundred years, so the presence of the ark of the covenant and the tabernacle as physical and visual assurances that God was with them was necessary to change their view of God and feel safe and free.

The yearly feasts

In Leviticus 23, God instituted seven yearly feasts for His covenant people. These used the material reminders of the tabernacle to help the people understand the ministry of the Messiah. All their senses were involved in the experience of the feasts, which gave their meaning even more impact.

Passover. God instituted the Passover in connection with His deliverance of Israel from Egypt (Exodus 11:1; 12:1–13:16). Each family of Israel was to choose a Passover lamb, kill it, and put the lamb's blood on the lintel and the two doorposts of their house and not go outside until morning (Exodus 12:21, 22). Scripture applies the blood of the Passover lamb to the Messiah: "Christ, our Passover, was sacrificed for us" (1 Corinthians 5:7). Those who had the blood of the Passover lamb on their doorpost were delivered (Exodus 12:27), as everyone who accepts the sacrificial blood of the Messiah will be saved from their sins (1 John 1:7). They were to eat the lamb with unleavened bread and bitter herbs (Exodus 12:8). At the last Passover Jesus spent with His disciples, He said, "Take, eat; this is My body"

(Matthew 26:26). He also said about the cup, "Drink from it, all of you. For this is My blood of the new covenant, which is shed for many for the remission of sins" (Matthew 26:27, 28). Thus, Scripture applies the Passover to the new covenant of the Messiah, Jesus Christ. The Feast of Unleavened Bread (Leviticus 23:6–8) started the day following Passover, so it continued the feast time. Exodus 12:15–20 makes it very clear that Israel was to have no leaven in their houses and they were not to eat anything that had leaven in it, and anyone who did would be cut off from Israel. Therefore, leaven seemed to be a symbol of sin, and the Feast of Unleavened Bread would be a fit symbol of the sinless Messiah (Hebrews 4:15).

Feast of Firstfruits/Pentecost. The Feast of Firstfruits was a celebration of the harvest, the time when the firstfruits of the harvest were to be given to the Lord (Deuteronomy 26:1–15). It was at Pentecost that the disciples were filled with the Holy Spirit (Acts 2:1, 4). The result was three thousand receiving the Messiah and being baptized that day (verse 41).

Passover and Pentecost were yearly feasts occurring in the spring. They symbolized the Messiah's pure life, sacrifice, and resurrection and the power of the Holy Spirit to proclaim the good news of salvation. They gave the Israelites hope for the appearance of the Messiah. These actions of the Messiah all happened while He was on earth or shortly after His ascension, thus fulfilling the salvific covenant promises. In the next chapter, we will see that the six infinitive phrases of Daniel 9:24 apply much of what these spring feasts symbolized.

Feast of Trumpets. Trumpets were used for many purposes in Scripture. The Feast of Trumpets seems to be connected to calling an assembly/convocation of the people (Leviticus 23:23–25; Numbers 10:2, 7). They were to make an "offering made by fire to the Lord" (Leviticus 23:25), indicating they were to confess and forsake their sins. During this feast, Israel was not to work but to make a "sabbath-rest" (Leviticus 23:24), thus focusing on their relationship with God.

Day of Atonement. The Feast of Trumpets took place ten days before the Day of Atonement as a preparation for that solemn occasion. To prepare for the Day of Atonement, the Israelites were to "afflict" their "souls" (Leviticus 23:27, 29, 32), which meant to humble themselves before God. It was a type of the Judgment; anyone in Israel who would not afflict, or humble, themselves before God would be "cut off from his people" (Leviticus 23:29).

The purpose of the Day of Atonement is found in Leviticus 16:29–34. The Israelites were to "afflict" their souls (verses 29, 31), indicating they faced judgment. Afflicting their souls by confessing and forsaking their sins (Isaiah 59:2) prepared them to be "at-one-ment" with God. The Day of Atonement was a day of cleansing for the sanctuary, priests, and people so that God could dwell with them. Leviticus 16:30 deals with the cleansing from sin: "For on that day the priest shall make atonement for you, to cleanse you, that you may be clean from all your sins before the LORD." Hebrews 9:24–28 applies what Leviticus tells us about the Day of Atonement to the Messiah's sacrificial and judicial roles that prepare for His second coming.

Feast of Tabernacles. Five days after the Day of Atonement was the Feast of Tabernacles (Leviticus 23:33–43). We have already seen that *tabernacle* means "dwelling place." This is why God wanted Israel to build a sanctuary/tabernacle—so that He could dwell with them. The Feast of Tabernacles symbolized the new heaven and new earth of Revelation chapters 21 and 22. Revelation 21:3 says, "I heard a loud voice from heaven saying, 'Behold, the tabernacle of God is with men, and He will dwell with them, and they shall be His people. God Himself will be with them and be their God.' " As we have seen in this chapter, Moses received directly from God information about how the sanctuary/tabernacle, its furniture, its services, the priests, and the feasts all illustrated God's everlasting covenant.

In Moses' day, the tabernacle was portable. This wilderness tabernacle was replaced by Solomon's temple during the approximately 850 years between Moses and Daniel. The Babylonian conquest in 586 B.C. destroyed Solomon's temple. The next two chapters look at the covenant in Daniel's generation and how Daniel's visions kept hope alive after the destruction of Jerusalem and the temple.

---

1. These figures arrived at by searching for these words in the *New King James Version* on Biblegateway.com.

2. *Easton's Bible Dictionary*, s.v. "Tabernacle," http://eastonsbibledictionary .org/3559-Tabernacle.php.

CHAPTER 4

Daniel's Prophecies Reveal
God's Authority and Covenant

S o far this book has looked at why and how covenants started due to our imperfect world not representing God's perfect ideal. Covenants are strategies for dealing with an imperfect world. In the generations from Adam and Eve down through Noah, Abraham, and Moses, the individual, local covenants God made with His people became a kind of heritage handed down to succeeding generations, with each needing a different strategy for dealing with their time in a changing, imperfect world.

Eve could not imagine evil because she had known only good. About fifteen hundred years after the Garden of Eden (roughly 2500 B.C.), the people in Noah's day couldn't imagine good because they had known mostly evil. About five hundred years after Abraham, Moses had to deal with his anger, his feelings of inadequacy, and often with a disobedient and murmuring people. By Daniel's day, some nine hundred years after Moses' time (roughly 600 B.C.), believing in covenants had become even more difficult. Covenants are complicated, and by Daniel's day, knowing who and what to believe, knowing how to keep the covenants that had been handed down, was even more difficult. By Daniel's time, Abraham's descendants were in captivity, and the promised Messiah was nowhere in sight.

In King Solomon's time, some four hundred years before Daniel (roughly 1000 B.C.), it seemed that the promises God had made to Abraham were being fulfilled in a grand way. Israel was a powerful nation, a great temple had been built, and the population was thriving. As a boy, Daniel saw Solomon's temple, but in 586 B.C., King Nebuchadnezzar's army destroyed that temple along with the city of Jerusalem. In this attack, the teenage Daniel and his friends were taken captive to Babylon.

Far from home and living in captivity, Daniel experienced personal, spiritual, and cultural isolation. After the heights of God's covenant with Abraham and Moses, after the glories of Solomon's temple and Jerusalem, the ruins of Daniel's former life and his present captivity in Babylon made the covenant seem more and more urgent but also more and more distant. However, Daniel still tried to keep his side of the covenant with God.

God also kept His connection with Daniel. In Babylon, Daniel and his friends held on to their Jewish faith, attracting the attention of King Nebuchadnezzar and later, after a regime change, King Darius (Daniel 2:28–49; 6:10–28). Daniel's close relationship with God helped him rise to be a trusted advisor because God spoke to him, giving him insights and answers that the king's other advisors did not have.

As a trusted advisor to Babylonian and Median kings of different faith traditions, Daniel was a somewhat unusual prophet. He never returned to Jerusalem, yet through his individual, local covenant, honored at a distance, this captive exile kept hope alive, receiving visions of the coming Messiah to lighten the dark present. Although Daniel's apocalyptic visions might seem confusing or strange, they gave more details about the covenant of the Messiah's coming than previous generations had received.

This chapter explores Daniel's visions. Of his visions, the most troubling aren't those filled with strange animals and confusing symbols; the one causing the most confusion and distress is the vision of the 2,300 days and the coming Messiah. This vision specifically mentions the covenant. This vision of the 2,300 days is a timeline for the promise and message of the Messiah's salvation through sacrifice (Daniel 9:4, 27). After some thirty-four hundred years, it might have seemed unbelievable to Daniel's generation, but prophecy was the best long-haul strategy for dealing with the hope-dimming impact of Babylonian captivity on the human beneficiaries of the everlasting covenant.

The book of Daniel emphasizes God's control over earthly kingdoms and His long-term covenant with His people, giving hope that the Babylonian captivity will not last forever. God is the Author of regime changes, whether Babylonian, Median, or Roman. For example, in chapter 2, Daniel interprets Nebuchadnezzar's dream of the image, foretelling the future kingdoms to be set up and brought down. This dream highlights how God changes leadership. Chapters 7 and 8 present a vision of competing animals, symbolizing a succession of earthly kingdoms that will seek to destroy covenant keepers like Daniel. In chapter 9, the angel Gabriel assures Daniel that God will bring an end to the Babylonian captivity. The first part of Daniel's timeline vision—the 2,300 days (Daniel 8:14)—tells him when Jerusalem will be rebuilt and when the Messiah will come to confirm the covenant originally promised to Adam and Eve (Genesis 3:15). The second part of the 2,300 days deals with the judgment, or the cleansing of the sanctuary (Daniel 8:14). When he had the timeline vision, Daniel did not understand what the 2,300 days meant (verse 15), so Gabriel came to explain to him that the second part of the timeline vision of the 2,300 days happens after Jerusalem is rebuilt and after the Messiah's sacrifice. Gabriel said: "The vision refers to the time of the end" (verse 17). God's messenger emphasized "the end" by stating the same thing again in a slightly different way: "I am making known to you what shall happen in the latter time" (verse 19). Therefore, Gabriel was saying that the end of the 2,300 days extended beyond the rebuilding of Jerusalem.

Daniel fainted and was sick for days (verse 27) as he thought about the "vision of the evenings and mornings" (verse 26), a reference back to the 2,300 days in verse 14. "The Hebrew words translated 'days' literally means 'evening mornings.' So the time period is 2,300 evenings and mornings."[1] Daniel was literally sick for days as he considered the timeline vision declaring "two thousand three hundred days; then the sanctuary shall be cleansed" (verse 14).

Even after Gabriel's visit, Daniel was still confused about the vision because, being a captive in Babylon, he could not see beyond the great need to rebuild Jerusalem and the temple or his desperate desire for the coming of the Messiah. Daniel tried to understand the vision by reading the writings of the prophet Jeremiah (2 Chronicles 36:21) "that He [God] would accomplish seventy years in the desolations of Jerusalem" (Daniel 9:2). Jeremiah's seventy years of desolation were well on their way to being finished, so Daniel was distressed to think that the timeline vision added 2,300 days to Jeremiah's seventy years.

God sent Gabriel a second time (verses 20–23) to explain the timeline vision to Daniel. These two explanations, along with the first part of Daniel's timeline vision, are the most complete Messianic prophecy in Scripture: "O Daniel, I have now come forth to give you skill to understand. At the beginning of your supplications the command went out, and I have come to tell you, for you are greatly beloved" (verses 22, 23). God sent Gabriel to Daniel because he was "greatly beloved." Twice in these verses, Gabriel assures Daniel of the Messiah's commitment to salvation and His desire for a relationship with Daniel's people (verses 25, 26). In verse 27, Gabriel promises that the Messiah will "confirm" His covenant.

Gabriel's explanation of the timeline vision gives us the dates of the rebuilding of Jerusalem and the Messiah's anointing and sacrifice.

Let's consider the context of Daniel's two-part timeline vision and Gabriel's two visits to explain it.

Because Gabriel's first explanation didn't make sense to Daniel, the prophet prayed in chapter 9, "with fasting, sackcloth, and ashes" (verse 3). Anxious to make sense of his timeline vision and Gabriel's explanation, Daniel claimed the promise of "God, who keeps His covenant and mercy with those who love Him" (verse 4). To this covenant-keeping, merciful God, Daniel confessed sins, setbacks, and unworthiness (verses 5–15). He feared that these sins might invalidate his prayers, but still, he pled that God would not lengthen the desolation of Jerusalem, calling God's attention to "Your sanctuary" and "Your people" (verses 17, 19). A desolate city, sanctuary, and people could not proclaim the Messiah's message or God's covenant, so Daniel urged, "Do not delay for Your own sake, my God, for Your city and Your people are called by Your name" (verse 19). Delay was not merely distressing for Daniel and for God's people; delay could actually cause people to lose hope in God and His covenant. Daniel wanted God's people to return home. The phrase "Your city Jerusalem, Your holy mountain" (verse 16) shows two concerns— the temple and the city of Jerusalem. "Your people" were also a major concern for Daniel, because they were in Babylon as captives.

God responded to Daniel's concerns by sending Gabriel a second time (verses 20–23). In verses 24–27, Gabriel's visit shows that God is both listening and keeping His covenant by sending the angel to answer Daniel's prayers in person.[2] In verse 24, Gabriel began his second visit by saying, "Seventy weeks are determined for your people and for your holy city." The "seventy weeks" are "determined," which means, in this context, "cut off" from something longer,[3] which in this case would be the "two thousand three hundred days" of Daniel 8:14 that Daniel was trying to understand. Gabriel reassured Daniel (and us) that God was not moving the goalposts of the covenant; the 2,300 days were not in addition to the seventy years of Jeremiah.

God answered Daniel, not by speeding up the timeline but by confirming His spiritual proximity across time and through the discomfort of what seemed like delay. Gabriel's words in Daniel 9:24–27 show that through prayer, God was personally close to His people as they awaited the rebuilding of Jerusalem and the Messiah's coming. Matthew 1:23 shows that Immanuel is the Messiah. It might seem that God was delaying, but Gabriel's message encouraged Daniel to remember that through prayer, God is still accessible. Though His people were in captivity far from the ruined temple and city of Jerusalem, Immanuel, "God with us," was still present with His people through prayer and Scripture until the Messiah's coming. And the same is true today; Immanuel is still "God with us."

After such a long delay, how would God's people know when the Messiah had come? How could they know whom to believe when it can be confusing to know who the Messiah is? Gabriel's second visit also gave Daniel a strategy for dealing with the difficulties of recognizing the Messiah, by helping Daniel and the readers of his book to think about what the Messiah would do. We will look at these things in the next chapter.

1. *Andrews Study Bible* (Berrien Springs, MI: Andrews University Press, 2010), Daniel Study Notes, s.v. "8:14 *For two thousand three hundred days*."

2. Referring to the prayer in Daniel 9:3–19.

3. *Andrews Study Bible*, s.v. *determined* Daniel 9:24 "*determined*."

CHAPTER 5

Daniel's Timeline Vision:
Messiah Fulfilling the Covenant

By the time Daniel received the timeline vision of 2,300 days, recorded in Daniel chapters 8 and 9, some thirty-four hundred years had passed since Adam and Eve first received God's covenant of a coming "Seed," the Messiah. All of God's covenant people had been looking for Him down through the ages. After such a long delay, how would God's people know when the Messiah had come? Recognizing the Messiah could be confusing. How could they know whom to believe?

In this chapter, we will find answers to these questions in Daniel 9:24–27, answers that give clear ways to identify the covenant Messiah and to understand what He was to do. Gabriel's second visit gave Daniel a strategy for dealing with these difficulties by helping Daniel and readers of his book to think about what the Messiah would do when He arrived.

A look at Gabriel's grammar gives unique insight into what the Messiah would do when He appeared. There are six infinitive phrases in Daniel 9:24. In English, a full infinitive includes the word *to* plus a verb—such as *to pray* or *to read*. The six infinitive phrases in Daniel 9 are *to finish*, *to make* (used twice), *to bring*, *to seal up*, and *to anoint*. The timing of the events to which these infinitives refer is open-ended, like God's covenant that continued from Adam and Eve to Noah, from Noah to Abraham, from Abraham to Moses, and from Moses to Daniel. Daniel's six infinitives look back to the promises of the covenant, but they also look forward to the future because they act as adverbs. Grammatically, adverbs answer such questions as where, when, how, why, how often, to what extent, and under what conditions an action takes place. Acting as adverbs, these six infinitive phrases answer *why* the Messiah is coming—He is coming to carry out God's purpose to fulfill the long-promised covenant. They also answer *to what extent* or *how thoroughly* the Messiah's coming will complete the purpose of the covenant. They give insight into the questions of *how* and *under what conditions* the Messiah will come by describing the situation existing at His coming and how He will deal with it. These actions will identify the Messiah. Let us look at these six infinitive phrases individually.

The first phrase, "to finish the transgression," states the Messiah's purpose—or one of the reasons *why* He is coming. Here the Hebrew word for *transgression* means "rebellious sin."[1] From the time Adam and Eve sinned in the Garden of Eden until the Messiah, every person on earth had committed the sin of breaking or rebelling against God's covenant, both intentionally and unintentionally. Gabriel told Daniel that the Messiah would be the first and only individual that would fully accept and keep God's covenant and that in Him, rebellion against the covenant and breaking it would stop.

The second phrase, "to make an end of sins," addresses the *why* question by stating another of the purposes of the Messiah's coming. Abraham had forgotten that it was up to the Messiah to fulfill the sacrifice prefigured by himself and his son Isaac, but Gabriel's message to Daniel assured him that God never forgets

His purpose in the covenant. To stop covenant rebellion and covenant breaking, the Messiah had to be the first person to live a sinless life since Adam and Eve rebelled against the covenant and broke it (Romans 3:23; Hebrews 4:15).

The third phrase emphasizes the second phrase by stating the same thing in a slightly different way, reemphasizing the sacrificial purpose—the *why*—of the Messiah's coming: "To make reconciliation for iniquity." Only the Messiah's sacrifice can reconcile God's people with the covenant and through this reconciliation, or atonement, fulfill the covenant (Romans 5:10).

The fourth phrase looks toward the future. "To bring in everlasting righteousness," the Messiah must live a life without sin. He "who knew no sin [became] sin for us, that we might become the righteousness of God in Him" (2 Corinthians 5:21). Gabriel told Daniel that the Messiah would live a perfect life that would enable Him to atone for our covenant breaking; He gives us His righteousness so that we can have everlasting righteousness. The Messiah also demonstrates what righteous covenant keeping is.

The fifth phrase, "to seal up vision and prophecy," answers two more *whys*, or purposes, of the Messiah's coming. "To seal" is to verify, confirm, or ratify all that the Scriptures have said about the Messiah as true. In the Messiah, all the Messianic prophecies would be confirmed, ratified, and verified—such as His virgin birth in Bethlehem (Micah 5:2) and the many details of His death (Psalm 22; Isaiah 53). Another purpose for sealing up the vision and prophecy is to make the Messianic prophecies both official and legally binding in their fulfillment of the covenant.

Gabriel's sixth phrase, "to anoint the Most Holy," answers *how* and *under what conditions* the Messiah's work as the Sacrifice and as High Priest would be carried out. The word *Messiah* means "anointed" or "anointed One." Anointing takes place at the beginning of someone's work. For example, a king is anointed at the beginning of his reign. A priest is anointed at the beginning of his priesthood. Anointing the "Most Holy" refers to the Most Holy Place in the sanctuary, which was originally the wilderness tabernacle constructed by Moses and later the temple in Jerusalem. The tabernacle is a place where God may dwell among His people (Exodus 25:8). Through the anointed Messiah, or Immanuel, God is "with us," both as the Sacrifice and as High Priest.

The term *Most Holy* refers to the Most Holy Place in the tabernacle and the temple where the high priest did his work annually on the Day of Atonement. The ark of the covenant was the only piece of furniture in the Most Holy Place. Inside the ark were the Ten Commandments; above the ark was the mercy seat where the high priest sprinkled the blood of the sacrifice, symbolizing the Messiah's sacrifice. Above the mercy seat was the brightness of God's presence (Exodus 40:34), surrounded by the wings of two cherubim. Unlike the annual work of the earthly high priest, the Messiah's self-sacrifice was to occur only once, when He "appeared to put away sin by the sacrifice of Himself" (Hebrews 9:22–28). Through His self-sacrifice, the Messiah embodied the mercy symbolized by the mercy seat; all the other sacrifices represented the Messiah's sacrifice that would take away sin. "To anoint the Most Holy" also referred to the Messiah as God's High Priest and God's sacrifice. The Messiah, like the tabernacle, is also the place where God is "with us" (John 1:14).

Grammatically, these six infinitive phrases could be interpreted as describing the responsibility of God's people who, since they had broken the covenant by not fulfilling their responsibilities, had been rejected by God and replaced. However, it is impossible for anyone other than the Messiah to accomplish the work of salvation through sacrifice or to model covenant keeping.

According to Gabriel's explanation and according to other Scriptures, the only one who could fulfill all six of these infinitive phrases was the Messiah, Jesus Christ. Some six hundred years after Gabriel's visits to Daniel, Peter said, "God anointed Jesus of Nazareth with the Holy Spirit and with power" (Acts 10:38). The disciple Mark testifies that at His baptism, Jesus witnessed "the Spirit descending upon Him like a dove. Then a voice came from heaven, 'You are My beloved Son, in whom I am well pleased' " (Mark 1:10, 11). Mark's testimony confirms Isaiah's prophecy about how God would acknowledge the Messiah:

> "Behold! My Servant whom I uphold,
> My Elect One in whom My soul delights!
> I have put My Spirit upon Him"
> (Isaiah 42:1).

After explaining how the Messiah would accomplish the work of salvation through sacrifice and by example, Gabriel broke down the "seventy weeks" for Daniel. To understand Daniel's timeline vision (in two parts) and Gabriel's two explanations, we need to understand that in apocalyptic prophecies, a day symbolizes a literal year.[2] In Daniel 9:25, the seventy prophetic weeks are broken into two periods—seven weeks and sixty-two weeks. Gabriel said,

> "Know therefore and understand,
> That from the going forth of the command
> To restore and build Jerusalem
> Until Messiah the Prince,

There shall be seven weeks and sixty-two weeks;
The street shall be built again, and the wall,
Even in troublesome times."

The period of seven weeks (forty-nine days of prophetic, symbolic time) is forty-nine actual years that would begin with "the command to restore and build Jerusalem" (verse 25). This command is found in Ezra 7:12, 13: "Artaxerxes, king of kings, to Ezra the priest, . . . I issue a decree that all those of the people of Israel and the priests and Levites in my realm, who volunteer to go up to Jerusalem, may go with you." That decree was made in 457 B.C. So Gabriel was telling Daniel that forty-nine years after 457 B.C., or in the year 408 B.C., Jerusalem would be rebuilt, reassuring him that God was going to keep His covenant.

The second time period of "sixty-two weeks" equals 434 prophetic days—or 434 actual years until Messiah the Prince. Adding the two time periods together, 49 years plus 434 years equals 483 years until the arrival of the Messiah, the anointed One. Counting 483 years following 457 B.C. brings this part of Daniel's timeline vision to its completion in A.D. 27 because there is no year 0. Jesus' baptism, His anointing by the visual sign of a dove alighting on Him (Mark 1:10; Luke 3:1, 21, 22; Acts 10:38), and the verbal sign of God's acknowledgment occurred in A.D. 27, just as prophesied in Daniel 9:25.

These first two time periods offered Daniel a timeline for the rebuilding of Jerusalem and for the coming of the Messiah. As Gabriel explained, the next part of the timeline vision foretold the time of the Messiah's sacrifice.

Gabriel continued his explanation to Daniel: "After the sixty-two weeks Messiah shall be cut off, but not for Himself" (verse 26). Being "cut off" refers to the Messiah's atoning death. Verse 27 told Daniel when the Messiah's sacrifice would take place.

The Messiah

> "shall confirm a covenant with many for one week;
> But in the middle of the week
> He shall bring an end to sacrifice and offering."

The phrase "confirm a covenant with many for one week" refers to the last week of the "seventy weeks."

Gabriel told Daniel that the covenant would be confirmed in this last week, the seventieth week of the timeline vision. The first sixty-nine weeks (483 years) ended, as we have seen, in A.D. 27. Therefore, this last week (seven actual years) extends from A.D. 27 to 34.

Gabriel went on to explain the time of the Messiah's sacrifice: "In the middle of the week He shall bring an end to sacrifice and offering" (verse 27). The Messiah would be "cut off, but not for Himself" (verse 26) in "the middle of the week," or between A.D. 27 and 34. Jesus' baptism occurred in the fall of the fifteenth year of Tiberius Caesar (Luke 3:1, 21), which was A.D. 27. Three and a half years later, at Passover in the spring of A.D. 31 (1 Corinthians 5:7), Jesus died on the cross as the "Lamb of God who takes away the sin of the world" (John 1:29; Hebrews 9:22). In doing so, Jesus fulfilled the prophecy of Daniel 9:24–27. He fulfilled the six infinitive phrases in Daniel 9:24 describing the Messiah's work, and He *kept His covenant*. Therefore, He brought "an end to sacrifice and offering" through the sacrifice He made on the cross. After the Messiah's sacrifice, it was no longer necessary to sacrifice lambs, because the "Lamb of God" had been slain (Revelation 13:8), fulfilling the atoning sacrifice of the everlasting covenant.[3]

Daniel 9:27 prophesied that the atoning sacrifice of the Messiah would take place in that last week of the seventy weeks (A.D. 27–34):

"He shall confirm a covenant with many for one week;
But in the middle of the week
He shall bring an end to sacrifice and offering."

Matthew 26:28 is the fulfillment of that prophecy: Jesus said, "For this is My blood of the new covenant, which is shed for many for the remission of sins" (Matthew 26:28). Jesus identified the cup of the Communion with a new covenant based on His blood "shed for many" on the cross. Both Daniel 9:27 and Matthew 26:28 are talking about God's covenant and His atoning sacrifice.

"He shall bring an end to sacrifice and offering" (Daniel 9:27). Jesus, the Lamb, made the ultimate sacrifice on the cross of Calvary, so animal sacrifices were no longer necessary. They had all pointed to the Messiah's sacrifice. God initiated animal sacrifices in the Garden of Eden after sin came in, but only the Messiah could end them by being the Sacrifice symbolized by all those other temple sacrifices.

There are some who look at the last part of Daniel 9:26 and 27 and have questions regarding whom the prophecy is talking about. If we understand the way Scripture and Jewish literature show contrast by a kind of "seesaw" poetry, there is no problem. This literary device is used throughout the Scripture. Notice, for example, Daniel 9:25. In the first part of the verse, we find what God does—He rebuilds Jerusalem. This is contrasted in the last part of the verse by what Satan does—he makes "troublesome times." In verse 26, Messiah's sacrifice in the first part of the verse is contrasted with Satan's war of desolations in the last part of the verse. In verse 27, God "confirms" His "covenant" in the first part of the verse, and Satan brings "abominations" in the last part of the verse. These contrasts show how Satan fights against God's covenant and

51

His covenant people.

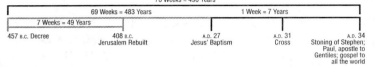

Daniel's timeline vision and Gabriel's two explanations are the most complete Messianic prophecy in Scripture. They brought hope to Daniel during dark times, reminding him, and us, that with the everlasting covenant, the best is still to come.

---

1. *Andrews Study Bible* (Berrien Springs, MI: Andrews University Press, 2010), Daniel Study Notes, s.v. 9:24 "*To finish the transgression.*"

2. Ezekiel 4:6; Numbers 14:34. Although *apocalyptic* is used these days to describe cataclysmic, end-of-days narratives, in ancient Greek, *apocalypse* (ἀπο-κάλυψις, *apokálypsis*) literally means "an uncovering," a "disclosure of knowledge," or "a revelation." Prophetic time can be apocalyptic in the sense that it discloses or reveals the timelines that are hidden in difficult prophecies.

3. The last week (of the seventy weeks) in Daniel 9:27 does not describe either the time of the end or the antichrist because there is no scriptural example of a break or gap in a timeline prophecy. As Gabriel shows Daniel, the last week (A.D. 27–34) is the heart of this Messianic prophecy that beautifully, accurately, and powerfully points to Jesus as the Messiah dying for our sins.

CHAPTER 6

Stephen and Saul/Paul: First-Generation Covenant Identity Crises

T he previous chapter showed how Daniel's timeline vision confirmed the covenant. Daniel's vision, received some six hundred years before the conclusion of the seventy-week timeline prophecy, outlined the rebuilding of Jerusalem, the coming of the Messiah, and the Messiah's sacrifice. In this chapter, we will see how the end of the seventy-week portion of Daniel's vision changed the leadership of God's chosen people from the Sanhedrin to the "Messiah the Prince" (Daniel 9:25) and from the earthly high priest, Caiaphas, to the Messiah, who was "cut off, but not for Himself" (verse 26).

We will also see in this chapter how the first generation of covenant keepers following the last prophetic week of Daniel's vision (starting in A.D. 34 with Stephen and focusing on Saul who became Paul) witnessed the covenant to Jews and Gentiles, fulfilling the promise that Abraham's descendants and all nations would be blessed by it. Through Paul's identity crisis (Romans 9–11) and his analogy of hope through the "olive tree," we will explore the challenges faced by this first generation of covenant keepers after the Messiah.

Although the Messiah brought hope, believing in Him also brought changes and challenges—for example, changes in worship. How should worship take place now that the Messiah's coming had put an end to the temple sacrifices that for so long had pointed forward to Him? How did the Messiah's role as High Priest affect earthly religious authorities? After waiting so long for the Messiah, why were religious authorities so upset by those who believed in Him? Who was in charge, anyway?

Young believers such as Stephen and Paul accepted Jesus as the Messiah and High Priest promised by the covenant, but now that He had returned to heaven, how were they to keep their covenant? Threatened by this generation of covenant keepers, the religious authorities were wary of their witness. If Eve and Adam had been so easily deceived in the Garden of Eden, shouldn't religious leaders be concerned about things that might seem a little too good to be true? Covenant keeping in the first generation after the Messiah was complicated, confusing, and sometimes dangerous.

Stephen, a young deacon in the local Jerusalem congregation, believed that Jesus was the long-awaited Messiah and was preaching the good news of the Messiah's coming and sacrifice with faith and power. Signs and wonders accompanied his witness, which shook the religious and political leadership (Acts 6:8–10). Stephen was brought before the council (verse 12) to be judged regarding his preaching about Jesus as the Messiah of the covenant. When he was given an opportunity to speak, he recounted the history of God's covenant, following it down the centuries just as we have done thus far in this book. From Abraham and the "covenant of circumcision," through Isaac, Jacob, and Joseph, Stephen pointed out how God had blessed and guided these patriarchs and His people. Stephen continued this same theme from Moses down to Solomon (Acts 7:2–47). Then, breaking off his narrative, he exclaimed, "I see the heavens opened and the Son of Man standing at the right hand of God!" (verse 56). These words, describing an amazing vision, were doubly explosive to the religious leaders. "Son of Man" was a term Jesus used to describe Himself (Luke 19:10), and His position standing at God's right hand placed Jesus in the position of the Messiah, challenging the authority of the Sanhedrin.

In Stephen's vision, not only was Jesus at the right hand of the Father, He was *standing* there (Acts 7:56). The young deacon saw Jesus standing at God's right hand—in contrast to the twenty-four times in Scripture when Jesus is described as *sitting* at the right hand of God. Standing at God's right hand denotes the Messiah is exercising His authority. Knowing the Scriptures, the religious leaders understood exactly what Jesus' position meant, and their reaction suggests that they understood Stephen's words as applying Daniel's prophecy of the "Messiah the Prince" (Daniel 9:25) to Jesus. The standing position suggested that Stephen believed that Jesus, as Messiah the Prince, was in charge of His people—not the Sanhedrin. The leaders understood that Stephen saw Jesus as the Sacrifice, or the "Messiah cut off, but not for Himself" (verse 26), and as the promised heavenly High Priest, "having become High Priest forever according to the order of Melchizedek" (Hebrews 6:20 quoting Psalm 110:4). Jesus is both the Sacrifice that the temple sacrifices pointed to and the heavenly High Priest that the earthly high priests, such as Caiaphas, merely represented.

Against both Jewish and Roman law, the Jewish leaders stoned Stephen in an effort to keep his declaration of the Messiah's coming from being heard. Their immediate and unlawful execution showed the extent to which the Sanhedrin understood exactly what Stephen was saying about Jesus. They did not want to accept Daniel's prophecy or Stephen's vision of the long-awaited Messiah because it could cost them their positions.

While Stephen was being stoned, a Jewish scholar observed from the sidelines and consented to Stephen's death. The record says, "The witnesses laid down their clothes at the feet of a young man named Saul" (Acts 7:58). Saul saw and heard everything Stephen said and did that day; he also attended the same synagogue as Stephen, so Saul was well acquainted with his message. Seeing Stephen's faith brought conviction to Saul.

Shortly after Stephen was stoned, Saul was struck down with light on his way to Damascus, and he heard Jesus' voice from heaven say, "It is hard for you to kick against the goads" (Acts 9:5). A goad is a long stick with a sharp point on the end, designed for driving cattle. Saul was fighting the conviction of the Holy Spirit, which was driving him to think like Stephen. Resisting it was like kicking against the sharp sticks used to prod animals and move them in the direction the herdsmen wanted them to go.

After his experience on the road to Damascus, Saul gave up fighting the Holy Spirit and answered God's call to lead out in taking the gospel to the Gentiles. Jesus the "High Priest"[1] had given the gospel commission to His disciples in Matthew 28:19, "Go therefore and make disciples of all the nations." In the apostle Paul's generation, covenant keepers carried the good news that the sacrificial part of the everlasting covenant has been fulfilled and that keeping the covenant was open to anyone. In the first generation after the Messiah, keeping the covenant meant going global—a going forth from Jerusalem to Judea, Samaria, and to the uttermost parts of the world (Acts 1:8).

But how do we honor the old faith and practices of the covenant while remaining open to new insights and practices? For some four thousand years, covenant keepers had wrestled with these questions as Jacob wrestled the angel (Genesis 32:24–30). In Paul's generation, the question became, How do we honor the identities that have shaped us as a family of covenant keepers descended from Abraham while also respecting new covenant keepers shaped by diverse identities and bringing them into the expanding family of Abraham? How does one live through an era that is both the end of something—such as the destruction of Jerusalem and the temple in Daniel's time, or the end of animal sacrifices after Jesus' death—and the beginning of something new—such as covenant keeping after the arrival and sacrifice of the Messiah or the expansion of Abraham's spiritual family to include all nations?

By the time he wrote the book of Romans, Paul had gone on two missionary tours and had almost completed his third. Like Daniel, Paul's sorrow and grief were not just for himself; they were for his people, both literally and spiritually. Just as Daniel was troubled about the future, Paul was troubled, in the first generation following the coming of the Messiah, by the collision of identities that was limiting the expansion of Abraham's spiritual family and causing sectarian dissent within it. Paul wrote, "I have great sorrow and continual grief in my heart" (Romans 9:2).

As a result of his experience on the road to Damascus, Paul, a Jew by birth and by religion, accepted Jesus Christ as the Messiah and Jesus' call to follow Him. The Lord also called Paul to be the apostle to the Gentiles (Romans 11:13). On his missionary tours, Paul reached out to Jews and to Gentiles, welcoming all into Abraham's extended family of covenant keepers. He saw that entry into Abraham's extended family, promised in Genesis 26:4, is not based on bloodlines; it is based on belief in Jesus Christ as the Messiah. "For you are all sons of God through faith in Christ Jesus. For as many of you as were baptized into Christ have put on Christ. There is neither Jew nor Greek, there is neither slave nor free, there is neither male nor female; for you are all one in Christ Jesus. And if you are Christ's, then you are Abraham's seed, and heirs according to the promise" (Galatians 3:26–29).

Opening Abraham's family to anyone who believed in Christ caused some to wonder whether Paul was somehow abandoning his Jewish heritage and faith or whether God had somehow abandoned His people.

Although Paul's ministry expanded to include Gentiles, his heart was with the Jews to the extent that he would have sacrificed his own salvation, if possible, for those who shared his lineage. He declared, "I could wish that I myself were accursed from Christ for my brethren, my countrymen according to the flesh, who are Israelites, to whom pertain the adoption, the glory, the covenants, the giving of the law, the service of God, and the promises" (Romans 9:3, 4). Paul gloried in the rich faith history of Israel's covenant with God. The law, the Ten Commandments, the ceremonial laws, and the other laws for godly living—all these were given to the Jewish people so they could share them with the world. Psalm 77:13 says, "Your way, O God, is in the sanctuary." God revealed His salvation, judgment, and prophecies of the future in the sanctuary. Of the many promises God gave to Israel, the most important ones were about the Messiah. These were precisely the promises Paul was trying to share with the world, updated by the recent coming and sacrifice of the Messiah.

Paul's sorrow and grief arose in part from the fact that some of his fellow Israelites did not yet see that the covenant had been updated by the Messiah's sacrifice. Paul wanted Israel to be saved. He wrote, "My heart's desire and prayer to God for

Israel is that they may be saved" (Romans 10:1). He summed up their situation in these words: "For they being ignorant of God's righteousness, and seeking to establish their own righteousness, have not submitted to the righteousness of God. For Christ is the end of the law for righteousness to everyone who believes" (Romans 10:3, 4). Some of the Jewish people were ignorant of how God could make them righteous.[2] They were trying to establish their own righteousness through works of the law. They did not accept the righteousness that Christ, their Messiah, had offered them through His perfect life and death.

To those who wondered, "Has God cast away His people?" Paul responded with an emphatic, "Certainly not! For I also am an Israelite, of the seed of Abraham, of the tribe of Benjamin" (Romans 11:1). Paul posed this question—"Has God cast away His people?"—to a congregation in Rome that was probably made up mostly of Gentiles. Even in Paul's day, some of the Gentiles seemed to think that with the expansion of Abraham's spiritual family, the Jewish people were being cast away or replaced by the Gentiles. "Certainly not!" Paul insisted and pointed to his own example as evidence that Israel had not been cast away. Paul wrote these words in A.D. 57, thirteen years after Stephen had been stoned in A.D. 34 and Paul had been called to be the apostle to the Gentiles.

At the end of the seventy-week prophecy of Daniel 9:24–27, there was a leadership change for God's people. Messiah replaced the Levitical high priest, and Messiah the Prince replaced the Sanhedrin. God's salvation was no longer demonstrated by the Levites sacrificing lambs in the temple in Jerusalem; it was demonstrated by the disciples going out to the world and telling of a crucified and risen Savior. In A.D. 34, all the followers of Jesus were Jewish. In Acts 1:8, Christ commissioned them to be His witnesses "to the end of the earth." From that time on, His covenant-keeping witnesses were composed of both Jews and Gentiles, not just the Jews.

Distressed at the mistaken belief that God would abandon His people, Paul emphasized the point that God had not cast away His people by repeating it in different words in Romans 11:2. "God has not cast away His people whom He foreknew. Or do you not know what the Scripture says of Elijah, how he pleads with God against Israel?" He then used Elijah's showdown with the prophets of Baal and Jezebel's death decree as an example of how Israel had forsaken God (1 Kings 19:14–18), but God did not forsake Israel.

Paul is sure that by extending the covenant to include Gentiles in Abraham's extended spiritual family, God has not forsaken Israel. Paul's writings show his deep engagement with the various identity crises that covenant keepers faced in that first generation after the Messiah's coming and sacrifice. In fact, Romans 9–11 can be read as a heartfelt exploration of these identity crises. It is not surprising that Paul, a scholar, quotes Scripture, but he does so prolifically. In the 90 verses of these three chapters, there are more than eighty Scripture citations, exclusive of the olive tree passage. Paul references other Bible writers as well as his own writings.

In their wide-ranging citations and impassioned arguments, chapters 9 to 11 can be read as a reflection of the complex identity crisis that Paul and other covenant keepers faced in the first generation after the Messiah's coming and sacrifice. Just as Daniel claimed God's promises when he was distressed about the timeline vision, Paul claimed the promises of Scripture, as if late in his ministry he was working his way through trouble spots and leaving a record for future covenant keepers who would face questions resulting from the identity crises of Abraham's extended spiritual family. "There is no distinction between Jew and Greek, for the same Lord over all is rich to all who call upon Him. For 'whoever calls on the name of the LORD shall be saved' " (Romans 10:12, 13).

Just as the timeline vision and Gabriel's visits comforted Daniel by confirming the rebuilding of Jerusalem and the temple and the coming and sacrifice of the Messiah, Paul's olive tree analogy gave hope for covenant keepers, whether Jew or Gentile.

Although Romans 9 to 11 reads like a collision of identity crises distressing the author, these three chapters also express hope through the organic metaphor of the olive tree.

"For the firstfruit is holy, the lump is also holy; and if the root is holy, so are the branches. And if some of the branches were broken off, and you, being a wild olive tree, were grafted in among them, and with them became a partaker of the root and fatness of the olive tree, do not boast against the branches. But if you do boast, remember that you do not support the root, but the root supports you" (Romans 11:16–18).

At first, the comparison of the firstfruits of the olive tree with a lump of clay from a potter's workshop might seem a bit odd, but this odd combination eloquently expresses the way covenant keepers might think Abraham's extended spiritual family was combining unlike and unrelated elements. The same Potter who created Adam from earth has created all the people encompassed by the everlasting covenant. To someone looking from the outside, the olive tree has a bit of an identity crisis, with wild olive shoots grafted into the native stalk, sharing the nutrients provided by the root that also supports the tree. Yet such diversity does not kill the olive tree; instead, it causes it to thrive and grow.

In Paul's generation, the question became, How do we honor the identities that have shaped us as a family of covenant keepers descended from Abraham, while also respecting new covenant keepers shaped by diverse identities and bringing them into the expanding family of Abraham? How does one live through an era that is both the end of something—such as the end of animal sacrifices after the death of Jesus—and the beginning of something new, such as covenant keeping after the coming and sacrifice of the Messiah or the expansion of Abraham's spiritual family to include all nations? Paul's answer: Be like the olive tree that thrives through the diverse identities grafted onto the olive root.

---

1. The book of Hebrews refers to Jesus as High Priest sixteen times.

2. See the fourth infinitive phrase in Daniel 9:24, "To bring in everlasting righteousness."

CHAPTER 7

Paul's Olive Tree and Abraham's Expanding Family Tree

Ironically, the author who spoke of an olive tree made up of native shoots, wild branches, and fallen branches, had been less tolerant in the past of the different covenant-keeping styles within the living descendants of Abraham's family tree. In his letter to the Galatians, Paul confessed to zealously persecuting his own people: "You have heard of my former conduct in Judaism, how I persecuted the church of God beyond measure and tried to destroy it. And I advanced in Judaism beyond many of my contemporaries in my own nation, being more exceedingly zealous for the traditions of my fathers" (Galatians 1:13, 14).

As Paul knew all too well, covenant keeping often goes hand in hand with covenant policing—or a tendency to label, demean, or hurt others who keep the covenant differently. In confessing his former behavior, Paul offered an opportunity for change and a hope for the future of Abraham's family tree through the analogy of the olive tree he introduced at the end of Romans 6. In this chapter, he discussed the Messiah as both the fulfillment and the root of God's covenant with Abraham and his descendants, whether Jew or Gentile. As we examine Paul's thinking in this chapter, we will clarify terms such as *the elect* and *the remnant* and discuss a few of the conflicts arising in this new generation of covenant keepers to whom Paul was writing.

The olive tree analogy is worth requoting:

> For if the firstfruit is holy, the lump is also holy; and if the root is holy, so are the branches. And if some of the branches were broken off, and you, being a wild olive tree, were grafted in among them, and with them became a partaker of the root and fatness of the olive tree, do not boast against the branches. But if you do boast, remember that you do not support the root, but the root supports you (Romans 11:16–18).

The "root" here in Paul's analogy is the same root that Isaiah prophesied would unite Jews and Gentiles:

> "And in that day there shall be a Root of Jesse,
> Who shall stand as a banner to the people;
> For the Gentiles shall seek Him,
> And His resting place shall be glorious"
> (Isaiah 11:10).

In Paul's generation of covenant keepers, the Messiah is the Root that both nourishes Jews and Gentiles and symbolizes belief in the coming and sacrifice of the Messiah. His resting place is both in heaven and in the hearts of covenant keepers, whether of Abraham's lineage or belonging to Abraham's extended spiritual family.

The olive tree in Romans 11:16–24 represents the saved, or "remnant" (Romans 9:27; 11:5), of Israel together with the saved of the Gentiles, "the wild branches" that were grafted in.

Paul writes, "For if the firstfruit is holy, the lump is also holy; and if the root is holy, so are the branches" (Romans 11:16). Notice that the word "holy" is used three times in this verse and is applied to "firstfruit," "lump," and "root." These three terms are used to illustrate Christ's work as the Root of the olive tree. In 1 Corinthians 15:20–23, Paul identifies Christ as "the firstfruits." Just as the Messiah is the Sacrifice to which all the animal sacrifices pointed, Christ is also the Offering symbolized by all firstfruit offerings.

The Greek word translated as "lump" means a "mass of things mixed together," which certainly applies to the mixture of branches and peoples found in the olive tree of Romans 11. Paul uses the word "lump" in Romans 9:21 to describe the raw materials from which the potter makes a "vessel for honor." In 1 Corinthians 5:7, Paul says "you may be a new lump" through "Christ, our Passover." Therefore, the "lump" is referring to the remainder of the Messiah's work. Paul uses the term "root" in Romans 15:12, referring to Isaiah 11:1 and 10, which speak of the "Root of Jesse," which is a Messianic prophecy that is also applied in Revelation 5:5 and Revelation 22:16. Paul concludes that since the root is holy, "so are the branches," because they are a part of the faith and salvation of the Messiah, who is the Root.

Romans 11:17 says, "Some of the branches were broken off, and you, being a wild olive tree, were grafted in among them, and with them became a partaker of the root and fatness of the olive tree." Why were some branches broken off? Verse 20 tells us: "Because of unbelief they were broken off." This shows that the branches on the tree are believers in the Messiah. Why were the wild branches grafted in the olive tree? Paul says that the wild branches were grafted in because of their faith—"You stand by faith" (verse 20). Notice that the wild branches "were grafted in among them [the natural branches], and with them became a partaker of the root and fatness of the olive tree." The two phrases "among them" and "with them" show Abraham's family expanding to include both Israel and the Gentiles as branches of the same olive tree.

In Romans 11:18–23, Paul warns the Gentile believers (wild branches), "Do not boast against the [natural] branches." "Remember," he warns, "that you do not support the root, but the root supports you." The faith tree began with God, and He used Israel, the Messiah, and the remnant of Israel to grow and sustain it. It did not begin with the Gentiles. "You will say then," Paul continues, " 'Branches were broken off that I might be grafted in' " (verse 19). This was another way of boasting that the Christian church, composed of both Jews and Gentiles, was better than or replaced, Israel. Remember, the tree was not cut down. Neither was a new tree planted nor were all the branches broken off. Paul's point to the Gentiles was, You have been grafted into a tree that was already established and that helps to sustain you. The branches that were broken off were broken off because of unbelief. In addition, he warns, "Do not be haughty, but fear. For if God did not spare the natural branches, He may not spare you either" (verses 20, 21). Those Gentile branches can and would be cut off unless "you continue in His goodness. Otherwise you also will be cut off" (verse 22).

In verse 23, Paul speaks about the natural branches that were broken off—those Jews who rejected Jesus as the Messiah. "And they also, if they do not continue in unbelief, will be grafted in, for God is able to graft them in again." The basis for being grafted into the tree, as well as for staying a part of the tree, is belief— faith. In verse 24, Paul explains why the natural branches can be grafted back in. "For if you were cut out of the olive tree which is wild by nature, and were grafted contrary to nature into a cultivated olive tree, how much more will these, who are natural branches, be grafted into their own olive tree?"

Paul makes a very interesting statement in verse 25. "I do not desire, brethren, that you should be ignorant of this mystery, lest you should be wise in your own opinion, that blindness in part has happened to Israel until the fullness of the Gentiles has come in." Paul did not want the Gentile believers to be arrogant and wise in their own opinion, thinking they were better than the Jewish people who did not believe. Paul says that Israel's blindness (or "hardening" in some translations) was only partial and that it would end when "the fullness of the Gentiles has come in." It seemed that bringing the gospel to the Gentiles was helped by the blindness (or hardness) of Israel. Yet at the end (the last people to be reached), God will remove Israel's blindness (or hardness), grafting all who believe into the tree.

Paul concludes his illustration of the olive tree in verse 26, "And so all Israel will be saved." In this context, "all Israel" refers to the totality of the tree—all the natural branches, the wild branches that have been grafted in, and the natural branches, once broken off but now also grafted back in. This is the remnant of Israel and the remnant of the Gentile church.

Rooted in the Jewish Messiah, Abraham's family tree expanded in Paul's generation to bless the nations. Covenant keepers who are grafted into the Messiah are the Israel that thrives through diversity. In verses 16–24, Paul uses an olive tree to illustrate the "remnant of Israel" and how they relate to Gentile believers. In this passage, notice that the tree is not cut down. Some (and only some) of the branches were broken off (verse 17). A new tree was not planted; wild branches (Gentiles) were grafted into the olive tree (verse 17). Also, the branches that were broken off can be grafted back into the tree (verse 23).

In verses 28 and 29, Paul says that although there were some in Israel who were enemies of the gospel, this still worked for the benefit of the Gentile believers. "Through their fall, to provoke them to jealousy, salvation has come to the Gentiles. Now if their fall is riches for the world, and their failure riches for the Gentiles, how much more their fullness!" (verses 11, 12). Even though God's promises and calling to Israel were irrevocable, each Israelite must accept by faith the salvation offered through the Messiah in order to be part of the remnant. This is why Paul twice refers to the "remnant" of Israel (Romans 9:27; 11:5), distinguishing the saved from the lost through belief in the Messiah.

Although it had been prophesied, the expansion of Abraham's family tree through the root of Jesse's line was perplexing both to the Jewish descendants of Abraham and to the Gentiles grafted into the Messiah's root. In Paul's generation, those who believed in the Messiah were often referred to as the church, set up as a kind of adversary against Israel in connection with the crucifixion of Christ.

Some incorrectly say the Christian church replaced Israel, either at the time of the Crucifixion or in A.D. 34. Matthew 27:1 says, "All the chief priests and elders of the people plotted against Jesus to put Him to death." The Bible tells us that the only reason John was able to get into the trial was that he had some connections with the high priest's family, and Peter was able to get in only because of John. It was a very small, handpicked mob that accused Jesus before Pilate. It was the corrupt leadership—or in Paul's analogy, a few broken branches—with a hired mob that plotted in the middle of the night to kill Jesus. There were some Jewish leaders, such as Nicodemus and Joseph of Arimathea, who were not part of that group. Nor were most of the Jewish people involved. Just prior to this, the masses were praising Jesus, putting palm branches on the path before Him, and singing hosannas. They were not plotting His death (Matthew 21:7–9).

There was a hired mob that agitated for Jesus' crucifixion. And the Jewish leaders came before Pilate and accused Jesus of violating the law. But the majority of the Jewish people were not clamoring for His death. When Pilate tried to find a way to save Jesus by offering His accusers a choice between Him or Barabbas, the leaders persuaded the hired mob to ask for Barabbas and to crucify Jesus (Matthew 27:20). Pilate saw "a tumult was rising"; he washed his hands and said he was innocent of "the blood of this just Person" (verse 24). Verse 25 says, "All the people answered and said, 'His blood be on us and on our children.' " In this verse, "all the people" were just the hand-picked, small, hired mob and the corrupt leadership who appeared before Pilate; it was not the mass of the Jewish people. The mob did not speak for all the people; they spoke only for themselves. Sympathetic to the weaknesses of the small, hired mob, Paul wrote, "For though He was crucified in weakness, yet He lives by the power of God. For we also are weak in Him, but we shall live with Him by the power of God toward you" (2 Corinthians 13:4).

Part of the power of the olive tree is that fallen branches can be reconnected to the life-saving tree. The mob cried, "His blood be on us and on our children," but in the Bible, bloodguilt is usually only on the guilty person—not on his family (Ezekiel 18:4, 20). Moreover, even in the few exceptions, the judgment fell only on the living family, not on the generations to come. Even the second of the Ten Commandments extends guilt only as far as the third and fourth generations (Exodus 20:5). So how could this mob's words bring guilt on endless generations of the Jewish people? Moreover, Jesus' prayer on the cross forgave those unwitting agents of His sacrifice—"Father, forgive them, for they do not know what they do" (Luke 23:34). Did God the Father answer His Son's prayer, or did He listen more to what the mob said to Pilate? Paul's olive tree analogy clearly shows his belief that broken branches (such as Paul himself, who persecuted Christians in his early career) can be reconnected to the Messiah who willingly came and sacrificed Himself to carry out a new chapter of the covenant for all.

In Paul's olive tree, Abraham's extended family of covenant keepers included Gentiles who were grafted into the tree along with Jewish branches and those broken branches, like Paul, that were grafted back in. It is not the branches but the root of the olive tree, the Messiah, that makes it holy: "If the root is holy, so are the branches" (Romans 11:16). Grafting in Gentile covenant keepers and regrafting broken branches into the olive tree fulfilled the ancient promise of the covenant by extending Abraham's family, starting at the end of the last week of Daniel's timeline vision in A.D. 34.

A look at Elijah or Isaiah or Stephen or Paul shows how covenant keeping tends to put a person at odds with those in political or religious authority. Listening to God's voice, especially when it runs contrary to political or religious leadership, can get covenant keepers into trouble and cause their own countrymen not to listen to them. For example, all four Gospels include a version of the statement that a covenant-keeping prophet is not accepted in his own country: "For Jesus Himself testified that a prophet has no honor in his own country" (John 4:44; Luke 4:24; Mark 6:4; Matthew 13:57).

In the long centuries after Paul, a primarily Jewish church later became a primarily Gentile church. What had been grafted together in Paul's olive tree split into separate structures. Dominant Christianity became identified with the Roman Catholic Church, while groups such as the Cathars, Waldensians, Huguenots, Lollards, and Hussites splintered off from the main body. Following the Reformation, other groups emerged, such as

Lutherans, Presbyterians, Anabaptists, Methodists, Adventists, and a whole host of other denominations.

In the transition from being primarily a Jewish church to becoming primarily a Gentile church, Christianity forgot its Jewish roots and its calling to extend Abraham's family. The church structure that emerged ignored Paul's inclusive voice and forgot his olive tree analogy. It lost sight of the fact that it is the Messiah's coming and sacrifice that makes the tree holy, not the religious authorities. Through the long, dark years of oppression, God's everlasting covenant was always with His covenant-keeping people, not with sectarian authorities.

From Adam to Jacob, from the time of Jacob until Solomon, from Rehoboam to Israel and Judah, from the Assyrian invasion down to A.D. 34, Abraham's family tree included his direct descendants who, like Paul, carried on the family line. Then with the coming and sacrifice of the Messiah, apostles such as Paul were called to extend Abraham's family of covenant keepers to anyone who believed in the Messiah's coming and sacrifice. Paul insisted, "If you are Christ's, then you are Abraham's seed, and heirs according to the promise" (Galatians 3:29). God is not limited to only one group that can reveal some part of His covenant. One of the reasons we have so many religious groups today is because many of them believe the covenants belong exclusively to them, but the covenant is God's olive tree into which anyone can be grafted.

Being a member of the "in" group is certainly very beneficial. During the times of the kings of Israel, a person would have been much better off and have a better chance of hearing truth, following truth, and being saved if they were a part of Judah as opposed to being a part of the northern tribes. The same principle applies to all ages and even today. As the olive tree analogy illustrates, the "in" group changes over time, but the root of the olive tree is stable and forgiving. If someone, like Paul, gets it wrong, he or she can be regrafted into the Messiah. "If they do not continue in unbelief, [they] will be grafted in, for God is able to graft them in again" (Romans 11:23).

As Paul shows through the olive tree, pride in one's status as grafted, natural, or regrafted is dangerous. "If you do boast, remember that you do not support the root, but the root supports you" (verse 18). Deserving recipients of the covenant and promises of God are not determined by "in" group status or by works; they are determined by the root of the olive tree, the Messiah. Almost all of the discussions about God's covenant revolve around which covenant keepers are God's true people, but God has no single group today who are "His people." Abraham's family tree was prophesied to expand to be a blessing to all nations. Jesus as the "High Priest" has commanded His disciples to go to "all the nations." Since the first generation after the Messiah, keeping the covenant has meant going global, carrying the good news of the gospel from Jerusalem to Judea, Samaria, and to the uttermost parts of the world (Acts 1:8). "There is neither Jew nor Greek, there is neither slave nor free, there is neither male nor female; for you are all one in Christ Jesus. And if you are Christ's, then you are Abraham's seed, and heirs according to the promise" (Galatians 3:28, 29).

If you believe in Christ, the Messiah, you are the seed of Abraham and an heir of the covenant promise. Paul was speaking to a primarily Gentile church when he said, "If you are Christ's, then you are Abraham's seed, and heirs" of the promise made to Abraham. The Messiah was at the heart of God's promises and His covenant with Abraham, so by being Abraham's seed, we are heirs. The Gentile believers were grafted into the olive tree of God along with the Jewish believers that pre-dated them. They grew with them and will be a part of them until Christ comes again. Therefore, in the olive tree we see a continuation, not a replacement, of God's covenant with His people.

Romans 11:26 states, "All Israel will be saved." Dispensation-alists teach that the Jewish people are the "all Israel" that will be saved because they believe that Israel is the recipient of the covenant both before the Cross and afterward. Will all Jewish people be saved, including Judas, Caiaphas, and a host of other wicked people? No, of course not.

Some who believe that this text refers to literal Jews interpret it to apply only to some point of time in the future when "all Israel will be saved." But for 100 percent of any people group to decide together to do the same thing would be more than miraculous at any time. The only way that could happen would be if God took away their free will, which He will not do.

On the other hand, replacement theology teaches that Israel was the recipient of the covenant before the Cross but has now been replaced by the Christian church. Thus the church is now Israel. But that is not what Paul said. Paul could have said, "All the church will be saved," but he did not. Let's apply the Romans 11:26 litmus test to "the church" and see how this theory stands up. Will all "the church" be saved? It depends to a great degree on one's definition of "the church." Catholics would probably say "the church" is the Catholic Church. Likewise, most church groups would probably identify their group as "the church." Will all Catholics or Baptists or Independents or Adventists or Meth-odists, and so on, be saved? Of course not. If "the church" means Christians, we could still ask, Will all who have professed Chris-tianity for the last two thousand years be saved? Of course not.

What we need to know is, Who is the "Israel" that Paul is speaking about when he says, "All Israel will be saved"? To know that we need to go back and look at the first time the term *Israel* is used in Scripture. Jacob had deceived his father and brother, forcing him to run to Laban's house, where he spent twenty years. When Jacob finally returned, his brother, Esau, came out with an army to meet him. Jacob humbled himself before Esau and God. Jacob wrestled with an "Angel" until the break of day when he was told, "Thy name shall be called no more Jacob, but Israel: for as a prince hast thou power with God and with men, and hast prevailed" (Genesis 32:28, KJV). From this text, as well as from the Hebrew language, we see that *Israel* means "a prince with God who prevails."

So who is "Israel"? Who is a prince with God who prevails? Jesus. Jesus is "the Prince of God" who has "prevailed" for us. He is the true Israel. Jacob, his twelve sons, and the nation of Israel were all foreshadows of the real Israel, the Messiah.

Matthew makes this very same connection between Israel and Jesus in Matthew 2:15 when he quotes a portion of Hosea 11:1, which says: "When Israel was a child, I loved him, and out of Egypt I called My son." When quoting this verse, Matthew identifies Jesus as the "Israel" mentioned by Hosea. Jesus is the fulfillment of Israel. Israel, like so many other things in Scripture, prefigured the Messiah.

If we define Israel (at least as it applies to Romans 11:26) as Jesus, then all those from the time of Adam until Jesus returns who "worship the Father in spirit and truth" (John 4:23), whether Jews or Gentiles, will be saved. We can say with Paul, Yes, "all Israel will be saved."

After Paul makes the powerful "all Israel" statement, he refers to Isaiah 59:20, 21 and Isaiah 27:9, saying,

> "The Deliverer will come out of Zion,
> And He will turn away ungodliness from Jacob;
> For this is My covenant with them,
> When I take away their sins."

He quotes from Isaiah's Messianic prophecies to validate the influx of the natural branches that will be grafted in at the end. The "Deliverer" (or "Redeemer" as some translations have it) is the Messiah who comes out of Zion. The promise is: "This is My covenant with them." God's covenant brings salvation through His everlasting covenant with Israel. The Messiah came through the nation of Israel and was the focus of that people's covenant with God. That is what Paul illustrated with the olive tree symbol, where Jesus as the Messiah is the tree, and Israel's remnant, believing people are the natural branches. The wild branches are believing Gentiles who were grafted into the olive tree with and among the other branches. In addition, the natural branches that were cut off of the olive tree must be grafted into it in order to be part of God's remnant people. Thus the entire tree represents the family of God throughout this earth's history. It is all the saved down through the ages with Jesus as the trunk and the branches intimately attached to Him (John 15:5). The tree will be totally complete at the end when the covenant is completed.

This is what we look forward to. We can hasten His coming by breaking down walls of separation and uniting all of God's children together in Him. For when the whole tree is full, then Jesus can come and complete the covenant. The analogy of the olive tree offers hope for the future of Abraham's expanding family tree.

CHAPTER 8

John's Woman of Revelation 12 and the Remnant Covenant Keepers

When the book of Revelation was written around A.D. 96, the author, who calls himself "John,"[1] might have felt as if the world was ending. There were conflicts inside the early church and outside. Isolated on Patmos, an island off the coast of Turkey, John had visions. In many ways, John's experience paralleled that of Daniel.

Daniel had seen Jerusalem destroyed in 586 B.C.; if John had not seen Jerusalem's destruction by the Romans in A.D. 70, he had heard of it at least. Daniel's timeline vision foretold the coming and sacrifice of the Messiah in A.D. 31, while John, according to the *Andrews Study Bible*, was one of Jesus Christ's disciples. Daniel, isolated in Babylon, awaited the Messiah's first coming. As a disciple, John had witnessed firsthand the coming and sacrifice of the Messiah foretold in Daniel's vision. Just as Daniel kept his covenant with God by looking forward to the rebuilding of Jerusalem and the coming of the Messiah, John kept his covenant by awaiting the second coming of the Messiah. Both Daniel and John received prophetic visions that gave them hope for the future, and they shared their hope through their writings. Perhaps the most important thing their prophecies did was to keep hope alive for Daniel and John through the long and uncertain years to come.

Like covenant keepers throughout history, Daniel and John were the remnant[2] for their generations. Whether Noah and his family, Abraham and his family, Moses, or Daniel and his friends, in each generation there have been three kinds of covenant keepers—those inside, those outside, and those broken off from established religions. As Paul's olive tree analogy shows, the remnant is anyone grafted onto the root, whether Jew or Gentile. Seeing the remnant not as an exclusive club but as a growing olive tree gives hope for the future. Broken branches, like Paul, can be reattached.

Unlike Daniel's timeline prophecy, John's prophecy of the woman in Revelation 12 has linear elements but is also a recurring story handed down to future covenant keepers living in a time when the work of the dragon, or serpent, to destroy takes a different shape. The woman's recurring story assures remnant covenant keepers that God values and loves them through the darkest times when the coils of the serpent, or dragon, threaten them. Like Paul's olive tree analogy, the woman in Revelation symbolizes the covenant keepers of each generation starting with Eve, whether inside, outside, or broken off from established religions. She represents covenant keepers who look for the Messiah's coming, wherever and whenever they are.

In the last chapter, we saw how the olive tree of Romans 11 represents the diverse believers encompassed by Abraham's extended family, including Jews and Gentiles, as people of the covenant. In this chapter, we will look at the woman of Revelation 12 who parallels but extends the olive tree analogy of Romans 11. The woman's recurring story, or prophetic loop, gives us hope as remnant covenant keepers in dark times.

Prophetically in Scripture, a woman is a symbol of God's

people. This was established right in the beginning when God addressed the issue of sin with Adam, Eve, and the serpent. God said,

> "I will put enmity
> Between you and the woman,
> And between your seed and her Seed;
> He shall bruise your head,
> And you shall bruise His heel"
> (Genesis 3:15).

In this text, the "you" is the serpent, Satan; "the woman" is Eve, representing God's people; "your seed" is Satan's people; "her Seed" is the Messiah; and "His" refers to the Messiah. This is the first Messianic prophecy in the Bible and it contains God's covenant with His people. The promise of a coming Messiah shows God's love for His fallen children. In addition, Genesis 3:20 says, "Adam called his wife's name Eve, because she was the mother of all living." Eve was the mother of the first natural born children on earth; therefore, she was the mother of all humanity, including the Messiah to come.

Later, the prophet Isaiah referred to a perpetual covenant of peace (Isaiah 54:10). Throughout this chapter, Isaiah referred to God as Israel's husband, a partner in fulfilling the covenant. Verses 5 and 6 say,

> "For your Maker is your husband,
> The LORD of hosts is His name;
> And your Redeemer is the Holy One of Israel;
> He is called the God of the whole earth.
> For the LORD has called you
> Like a woman forsaken and grieved in spirit,

Like a youthful wife when you were refused," says your
   God.

God's acceptance shows kindness and love to a woman who
has been mistreated or rejected by others; He sees her value when
others do not. The Messiah "your Redeemer" who is "the Holy
One of Israel" promises to meet all of her needs.

Jeremiah 3:14 and 20 and 6:2 also compare Jerusalem (Zion)
to a woman. Second Corinthians 11:2 refers to God's people
after the time of the Cross as a woman. "For I am jealous for you
with godly jealousy. For I have betrothed you to one husband,
that I may present you as a chaste virgin to Christ." Here Paul is
describing the Corinthian covenant keepers as a "betrothed" and
"chaste virgin" presented to Christ, her future Husband.

These verses apply to the woman of Revelation 12, where the
woman also appears as a symbol of God's people. Just as Eve symbolizes God's people at the beginning of Scripture, the woman of
Revelation symbolizes His people at the end of Scripture.

It is worth quoting the woman analogy of Revelation 12 in
full.

Now a great sign appeared in heaven: a woman clothed
   with the sun, with the moon under her feet, and on her
   head a garland of twelve stars. Then being with child, she
   cried out in labor and in pain to give birth.

And another sign appeared in heaven: behold, a great, fiery
   red dragon having seven heads and ten horns, and seven
   diadems on his heads. His tail drew a third of the stars
   of heaven and threw them to the earth. And the dragon
   stood before the woman who was ready to give birth, to
   devour her Child as soon as it was born. She bore a male
   Child who was to rule all nations with a rod of iron. And

her Child was caught up to God and His throne. Then the woman fled into the wilderness, where she has a place prepared by God, that they should feed her there one thousand two hundred and sixty days. . . .

Now when the dragon saw that he had been cast to the earth, he persecuted the woman who gave birth to the male Child. But the woman was given two wings of a great eagle, that she might fly into the wilderness to her place, where she is nourished for a time and times and half a time, from the presence of the serpent. So the serpent spewed water out of his mouth like a flood after the woman, that he might cause her to be carried away by the flood. But the earth helped the woman, and the earth opened its mouth and swallowed up the flood which the dragon had spewed out of his mouth. And the dragon was enraged with the woman, and he went to make war with the rest of her offspring, who keep the commandments of God and have the testimony of Jesus Christ (Revelation 12:1–6, 13–17).

Like the rainbow for Noah or the olive tree for Paul, the woman of Revelation 12 embodies God's covenant, spanning heaven and rooted in the earth. The sun fitly symbolizes God's people clothed in Christ's righteousness (Matthew 5:14). In Paul's words, "For as many of you as were baptized into Christ have put on Christ" (Galatians 3:27). The moon reflects the light of the sun, and God's people stand on the Word of God, which reflects "the Word [who] became flesh and dwelt among us" (John 1:14). The twelve stars symbolize the twelve tribes of Israel.[3]

Like the union of the diverse branches that produce olives in Paul's olive tree analogy, the union between God and His people has been productive. The linear elements parallel the story of the

Messiah's coming into the family line of Abraham by His birth through Mary, who was a direct descendant. As prophesied from Genesis to Isaiah to Daniel to Hosea, the Messiah came through the nation of Israel. After Jesus' birth, Mary and Joseph fled to Egypt with the Infant, because Satan (the serpent in Genesis and the dragon in Revelation) used Herod to kill all the male children under two years old in Bethlehem in an attempt to "devour the Child as soon as it was born" (Matthew 2:16–18). Like Mary, the woman "bore a male Child who was to rule all nations with a rod of iron." This is a clear reference to Jesus as the fulfillment of the Messianic prophecy in Psalm 2:7–9 that mentions ruling with a "rod of iron." In Revelation 19:15 and 16, John borrows this language to describe the Messiah. Like Mary's Child, the woman's Child ascended to heaven as recorded in Acts 1:8 through 11. Still menaced by the dragon, the woman flees to a place of safety in the wilderness.

This narrative is repeated in the woman's recurring story and prophetic loop. When Satan can no longer get at Christ directly, time after time he goes after remnant covenant keepers, symbolized by the woman who flees into the wilderness in each generation when the dragon's work to destroy takes a different shape.

The woman's recurring story and prophetic loop cannot refer only to Israel (the nation of Israel) before the birth of Jesus and then only to the church (Gentile Christians) afterward. It is the same woman. She does not change; she is not two different women. It cannot refer only to the nation of Israel, because within a few years of the Child's ascension, the nation of Israel ceased to exist for close to two thousand years, yet the woman continues to be persecuted after the Child ascends to His throne.

In some ways, it seems the woman's recurring story and

prophetic loop could apply only to the Jewish people, but the woman loops back to the Garden of Eden. Through Mary, the Messiah was a direct descendant of Abraham, and the Jewish people were persecuted after Jesus ascended. But the account in Revelation 12 does not go back only to Judah, son of Jacob/Israel (the first Jewish person). The woman goes all the way back some two thousand years before the first Jewish person was born. When the serpent came to the Garden of Eden after being thrown out of heaven, he subtly attacked Eve, the first woman (Genesis 3:15).

The woman's recurring story and prophetic loop cannot refer only to the church as we understand churches, because they were not around before the Child was born and because what became the historical church forgot its Jewish roots and eventually excluded and persecuted Jewish believers.[4]

Both the very first Messianic prophecy and the very first covenant were made through women. The first covenant was with Eve and all her "Seed," or descendants, down to the time of Mary, mother of the Messiah. That first covenant of the Messiah's coming and sacrifice is the basis for God's everlasting covenant. Daniel's timeline vision foresaw the Messiah's first coming and sacrifice, while John's vision of the woman of Revelation 12 foresees the Messiah's second coming. The woman is the same woman before she gives birth and after she gives birth. Just as in Romans 11, there was no new olive tree that was planted, no other woman steps into the recurring story and prophetic loop to replace the woman who gave birth to the Child. The woman is God's people before Jesus was born, and she also represents God's people after the ascension. In the olive tree, "all Israel will be saved," both Jews, grafted-in Gentiles, and reattached branches; likewise, the woman also represents all covenant keepers who believe in the coming and sacrifice of the Messiah and who look forward to His return.

In each generation, Satan's recurring strategy has been to divide God's remnant people, represented by Paul's olive tree and by the woman of Revelation 12, by getting them to fight or persecute each other. Saul/Paul persecuted his fellow believers. Christianity persecuted the Jews. Christians persecuted other Christians. Satan first divided the church between Jews and Gentiles. Then he divided the Jews from each other and Gentiles from each other.

Three things brought separation between the Jewish and Gentile believers in the early church from the second through the fourth centuries. First, the change of the Sabbath from Saturday to Sunday. Second, separation of clergy and laity, in which the clergy had all the authority and were the only ones authorized to preach the gospel and interpret the Scriptures. Third, replacement theology, which taught that the Christian church had replaced Israel so that all the covenants, promises, and blessings of Israel belonged now to the church. This thinking was bolstered also by pointing to the Jews as having been instrumental in Christ's death. The church unfairly blamed the Jewish people, although Pilate had final authority. If Christ had been killed against His will, He could not have fulfilled the covenant (Isaiah 53:4–6). If the Messiah had not willingly sacrificed Himself, He could not have fulfilled Daniel's time-line vision that "Messiah shall be cut off, but not for Himself" (Daniel 9:26). Like Daniel, John also shows the voluntary nature of the Messiah's sacrifice: "You were slain, and have redeemed us to God by Your blood out of every tribe and tongue and people and nation" (Revelation 5:9).

Other factors were instrumental in dividing Jewish and Gentile believers in the early church. During the time of the Roman Empire, the Romans considered Christians to be a sect of the

Jews. Since many Jews rebelled against Rome, Christians wanted to separate themselves from the Jews so they would not be persecuted with them for their rebellion against the empire. In the second century, Gentiles outnumbered Jews in the church. This made it easier to change the Sabbath from Saturday to Sunday, although most Jews would not accept the change. When Emperor Constantine made a deal with church leaders to declare Christianity the official religion of the empire, the church had to make compromises, including worshiping on Sunday. Replacement theology and the division between clergy and laity helped facilitate the change of the Sabbath from Saturday to Sunday. Over the generations, Satan has also used doctrinal issues, false teachings, worship styles, and leadership styles to divide and cause fighting and persecution among Jewish and Gentile[5] believers.

In spite of the floods of persecution (Revelation 12:15) both within and without the church, remnant covenant keepers, symbolized by the olive tree in Romans 11 and the woman in Revelation 12, have overcome and thrived in all generations. In the prophet Elijah's day, for example, he confessed to God that the religious and political leadership had "forsaken Your covenant, torn down Your altars, and killed Your prophets with the sword" (1 Kings 19:10, 14). However, Elijah and a remnant of seven thousand people "whose knees have not bowed to Baal" (1 Kings 19:18; Romans 11:4) kept their covenant with God. From Eve to Mary, from Noah to Abraham, from Daniel to Paul, from Paul to John, and beyond—the remnant of Israel have salvation because they have accepted the grace of their Messiah. As Paul says in Romans 9:27, "Though the number of the children of Israel be as the sand of the sea, the remnant will be saved." This is what Paul refers to in Romans 11:5 as "a remnant according to the election of grace." Although Satan has used floods of persecution to try to destroy the covenant-keeping remnant, through the woman's recurring story and prophetic loop, John gives hope to future generations: "Do not fear any of those things which you are about to suffer. Indeed, the devil is about to throw some of you into prison, that you may be tested, and you will have tribulation ten days. Be faithful until death, and I will give you the crown of life" (Revelation 2:10).

The woman's recurring story and prophetic loop look forward to God's completion of the everlasting covenant by reminding readers of the long history of the covenant in Scripture. Covenants came about as strategies for helping remnant covenant keepers deal with an imperfect world. God's everlasting covenant was, and is, God's commitment to salvation through the Messiah and His desire for an eternal, loving relationship with His people like He had with Adam and Eve before the serpent and sin. Through the long years between His promise to Adam and Eve and the coming and sacrifice of the Messiah, God made covenants across the generations. His covenant in Moses' day, around 1440 B.C., was to construct both a tabernacle and the furniture that included the ark of the covenant.

Located in the Most Holy Place in the tabernacle and later in the temple, the ark of the covenant embodied God's everlasting covenant. Inside it were the Ten Commandments showing God's justice. On top was the mercy seat showing God's mercy. Above the mercy seat was the glory of God, and the two cherubim over the ark symbolized God's presence. Like the tabernacle, the ark of the covenant was an earthly symbol of God's heavenly throne, but it wasn't just a symbol. The tabernacle was a place where God could dwell among His people (Exodus 25:8), and the ark of the covenant was God's earthly throne within the tabernacle. Once a year, on the Day of Atonement, the high priest sprinkled the blood of the sacrifice on the mercy seat, which symbolized the sacrifice of the Messiah. Ten days before the Day of Atonement all Israelites were to confess and forsake their sins, and anyone who refused to do so was cut off. The "rest," or "remnant," of God's people entered into "at-one-ment" with God. Atonement comprises both the sacrifice and the relationship of the everlasting covenant.

The remnant covenant keepers who most fully represent the Messiah and have a loving relationship with Him are the ones who draw Satan's greatest anger as they await the Messiah's return. John describes the remnant covenant keepers with two phrases—those "who keep the commandments of God" and those who also "have the testimony of Jesus Christ" (Revelation 12:17).

The first phrase describes the remnant as those who keep the Ten Commandments, which are the constitution of God's government; all His other laws or commands are based on them. God Himself spoke and wrote them with His finger (Exodus 20:1–17; 31:18), and they were kept in the ark of the covenant. Jesus said, "If you love Me, keep My commandments" (John 14:15). God shows His love by inscribing His laws in the minds and hearts of covenant keepers: "This is the covenant that I will make with the house of Israel after those days, says the LORD: I will put My laws in their mind and write them on their hearts; and I will be their God, and they shall be My people" (Hebrews 8:10). Having God's law written in their minds shows that the remnant think like the Messiah. "Let this mind be in you which was also in Christ Jesus" (Philippians 2:5). In writing His law in our minds and hearts, God reminds forgetful humans of the salvation that the Messiah gives us. He also says we will show our love by willingly keeping His commandments in a loving covenant relationship.

The second characteristic of the remnant of Revelation 12:17

is that they "have the testimony of Jesus Christ." John joins the two phrases with the conjunction "and"—those "who keep the commandments of God and have the testimony of Jesus Christ" (Revelation 12:17). The remnant are not identified with only one or the other—but with both. Revelation 14:12 is a parallel verse to Revelation 12:17. It says, "Here is the patience of the saints; here are those who keep the commandments of God and the faith of Jesus." In context, the "saints" refer to those who are alive and are saved when Jesus comes (Revelation 14:15, 16). Here, we see the same two characteristics stated in Revelation 12:17—the remnant will be keeping God's commandments, *and* they will have "the faith of Jesus." The text does not say "faith *in* Jesus," but "the faith *of* Jesus." God's last-day remnant will have the same faith that the Messiah had when He was in the Garden of Gethsemane and prayed, "Not as I will, but as You will" (Matthew 26:39). It will not be our covenant or promises to God that will bring our generation through the woman's recurring story and prophetic loop but God's covenant lived out in us.

The woman's prophetic loop is connected to other linear timelines, such as Daniel's timeline vision of the 2,300 days. In chapter 3, we explored the first part of Daniel's timeline vision and Gabriel's two explanations. The second part of Daniel's timeline vision is explained in John's vision of the three angels of Revelation 14:6–12. Their messages are a wake-up call that the judgment and the cleansing of the sanctuary have started. Let's look at the three angels' messages. To anyone who has fallen asleep, it's time to wake up and be sure you're in harmony with the covenant.

The first angel's message is divided into five points. Point one is the "everlasting gospel" that is proclaimed "to every nation, tribe, tongue, and people." This is the completion of the work started at the end of Daniel's seventy weeks in A.D. 34, when

Stephen was stoned and Paul became the apostle to the Gentiles.

The second point of the first angel's message is: "Fear God"; that is, respect and honor Him. The olive tree and the woman are identified by their covenant keeping, specifically keeping the commandments and having faith in the Messiah even through difficult times.

The third point is "give glory to Him." Glorifying God means living such a virtuous life that covenant keepers will reflect God's glory on earth as described in Matthew 5:16, "Let your light so shine before men, that they may see your good works and glorify your Father in heaven."

Point four is: "the hour of His judgment has come." This is the end of the second part of Daniel's timeline vision, the final Day of Atonement when all God's people are judged.

Point five is "worship Him who made heaven and earth, the sea and springs of water." For anyone who has forgotten that their

> "Maker is [their] husband;
> The LORD of hosts is His name;
> And [their] Redeemer is the Holy One of Israel;
> He is called the God of the whole earth"
> (Isaiah 54:5)

and that the Sabbath is like a wedding band that symbolizes marriage, it's time to remember that keeping His Sabbath holy proclaims that we are in a covenant relationship with God.

The wake-up call of the second angel says, "Babylon is fallen" (Revelation 14:8). The woman who symbolizes the fall is the reverse of the woman in Revelation 12. The woman of Revelation 17 did not escape the dragon. Like Eve, she was deceived, but her deception is double. Satan uses both persuasion and wine to make her forget her covenant. Unable to think clearly, the woman of Revelation 17 encourages others to partake (Revelation 17:2). The wine she has drunk is a mixture of half-truths and lies. In her drunken state, she cannot choose to have God's laws in her heart and mind, so Satan's message is written on her forehead (Revelation 17:5). Her wake-up call has a follow-up in Revelation 18:4. "Come out of her, my people, lest you share in her sins, and lest you receive of her plagues." The second angel's wake-up call shows that God has people everywhere in the "Babylon" (Revelation 17:5) of religious and political confusion. Like the woman of Revelation 17, they are drunk and forgetful of the truth of His everlasting covenant.

The third angel's wake-up call is related to the second: "If anyone worships the beast and his image, and receives his mark on his forehead or on his hand, he himself shall also drink of the wine of the wrath of God" (Revelation 14:9). Marks in the forehead or hand indicate Satan's deception and coercion.

The remnant covenant keepers who wake up are "those who keep the commandments of God and the faith of Jesus" (Revelation 14:12). They are ready for the judgment and the Messiah's coming (Revelation 14:13–20).

Both Paul's olive tree in Romans 11 and John's woman of Revelation 12 symbolize God's people, or the extended family of Abraham, who are the remnant covenant keepers. In the first generation after the Messiah, keeping the covenant meant going global, a going forth from Jerusalem to Judea, Samaria, and the uttermost parts of the world (Acts 1:8). After the Messiah's first coming, Abraham's family was opened to Gentiles who believed in the Messiah. The coming and sacrifice of the Messiah also brought a new way of thinking about the remnant, identifying them as those covenant keepers who believe in Christ. In the olive tree and in the woman of Revelation, believers are united in the Messiah's first coming and living toward the promise of His return. John's three angels of Revelation 14 remind the remnant covenant keepers to wake up and be ready for the Messiah's return.

---

1. The *Andrews Study Bible* suggests "early historical sources identify him with the John of the Gospels, brother of James, son of Zebedee, a disciple of Jesus (Matt. 4:21–22; 17:1; Mark 3:17; 10:35–41; Luke 9:28, 54; 22:8; John 13:23–25; 18:15–17)." This source also remarks on a stylistic similarity between the book of Revelation and the Gospel of John. "The Revelation of Jesus Christ: Author," *Andrews Study Bible* (Berrien Springs, MI: Andrews University Press, 2010).

2. The King James Version of Revelation 12:17 uses the word "remnant" where the NKJV uses the word "rest".

3. *Andrews Study Bible*, Revelation Study Notes, s.v. "12:1 *twelve stars*."

4. For information on how Satan worked to destroy Jewish covenant keepers with floods of persecution, see Dr. Alexander Bolotnikov's insightful and scholarly paper *Mission From the Remnant to the Remnant*, forthcoming. Dr. Bolotnikov has generously given permission to cite both his forthcoming article and some of his work that is also available through the Shalom Learning Center, http://www.shalomlc.org.

5. Christians did not face the magnitude of systemic persecution that the Jews did. At various points, nonconformists or heretics were sporadically persecuted both before and after the Reformation; for example, the Cathars, Waldensians, Huguenots, Lollards, Hussites, Lutherans, Presbyterians, Anabaptists, Puritans, Quakers, and Methodists. The severity of punishment and persecution differed across Europe. The abuses of organized religion were connected to political changes, for example the English king Henry VIII's break with Rome or during the French Revolution when Pope Pius VI was taken captive during efforts to de-Christianize the country.

God's Covenant Completed?

When will God's covenant be completed? No one knows when the Messiah will come again to complete His covenant (Matthew 24:36). John's three angels of Revelation 14:6–12 remind us, as remnant covenant keepers, to stay ready by keeping God's laws written in our minds and hearts. Also, we must be ready for His coming by keeping faith with the Messiah through a loving relationship with Him.

In chapter 1, we discovered that covenants are necessary because imperfection marred God's perfect creation. Adam and Eve fell for a con job in the Garden where there were only two competing voices—God's voice and the serpent's voice. Our confusing world is full of competing voices, and it can be hard to know who and what to believe in. It's easy to look back and judge Eve and Adam, but today we deal with some of the same kinds of difficulties they faced, and understanding how covenants came about can remind us of the serpent's modus operandi, which he still uses. His deception and sabotage remind us that, like Eve, we can be deceived into breaking our covenant with God.

Chapter 2 discussed Abraham, whose faith led him to the cusp of sacrificing his own son. When Abraham finally looked up, he saw a ram in the thicket. God provided the ram because covenants are complicated. In doing so, He helped Abraham deal with his side of the covenant. Through the ram, God reminded Abraham and Isaac that they prefigured but could never complete the work of salvation through sacrifice. Only God and the Messiah could do that.

Chapter 3 dealt with how God delivered Israel from Egypt through a reluctant Moses. Then God spoke and wrote the Ten Commandments as a basis for understanding the covenant and our relationship with both Him and our fellow human beings. On Mount Sinai, God gave Moses the plans and instructions for building the sanctuary/tabernacle and its furniture, along with instructions about its services—all of which were symbolic of the life and ministry of the Messiah. God gave Moses seven yearly feasts for His covenant people (Leviticus 23). The yearly feasts also illustrated the Messiah's ministry and will culminate with His return and kingdom (Leviticus 23; Revelation 21:1–5).

In chapter 4, we saw Daniel far from home and living in captivity. Daniel experienced personal, spiritual, and cultural isolation. After the heights of God's covenant with Abraham and the glories of Solomon's temple and Jerusalem, the ruins of Daniel's former life and the difficulties of his present life in Babylon made the covenant seem more and more urgent but also more and more distant. However, Daniel still tried to keep his side of the covenant with God. Some thirty-four hundred years after the covenant of Genesis 3:15, it might have been difficult for Daniel and his contemporaries to continue trusting God's covenant, but prophecy was their best long-haul strategy for dealing with the hope-dimming impact of the Babylonian captivity. They were still beneficiaries of the everlasting covenant.

Chapter 5 explored the first part of Daniel's timeline vision and Gabriel's two explanations, which together make up the most complete Messianic prophecy in Scripture. Daniel's prophecy confirmed that the Messiah would come through the nation of

Israel and that He was the focus of the covenant. This brought hope to Daniel during dark times, reminding him, and us, that with the everlasting covenant, the best is still to come.

Chapter 6 considered how in the first generation after the Messiah's coming and sacrifice, the question became, How do we honor the identities that shape us as a family of covenant keepers, descended from Abraham, while respecting new covenant keepers shaped by diverse identities and accepting them into the expanding family of Abraham? How does one live through an era that is both the end of something and the beginning of something new—like covenant keeping after the coming and sacrifice of the Messiah or the expansion of Abraham's spiritual family to include all nations? Paul's answer? Be like the olive tree and thrive through the diverse identities grafted into the olive root.

Chapter 7 showed that the Messiah came through the nation of Israel and was the focus of their covenant. That is what Paul illustrated with the olive tree symbol, where Jesus, as the Messiah, is the tree, Israel's covenant-keeping remnant are the natural branches, and the wild branches are the believing Gentiles who were grafted into the olive tree among the other branches. In addition, the natural branches that were cut off the olive tree must be grafted into it to be part of God's remnant people.

Chapter 8 focused on John's woman of Revelation 12, symbolizing God's people, or the extended family of Abraham who are the remnant covenant keepers. After the Messiah's first coming, Abraham's family was opened to Gentiles who believed in the Messiah. The coming and sacrifice of the Messiah also brought a new way of thinking about the remnant, defined as those covenant keepers who believe in Christ. In the olive tree and in the woman of Revelation 14, believers are united in the Messiah's first coming and live lives focused on the promise of His return.

Covenant? By using the old-fashioned word *covenant*, this book has shown that one way to stay ready for the Messiah's second coming is to think about our relationship with God as a covenant. Like the covenant of marriage, which is an example used many times in Scripture to show God's relationship to His people, our covenant with God needs ongoing attention and commitment.

God wants us to believe what is hard for us to believe. God's love for us is beyond our comprehension (John 3:16). He wants to spend eternity with us in a loving relationship, in a perfect, beautiful environment. That is the intended result of the everlasting covenant (Revelation 21:1–27; 22:1–21). God's remnant are those who enter into His covenant and who will experience the completion of that covenant. Today and for eternity, anyone can experience the results of God's everlasting covenant.

Do you want to experience the completion of God's covenant in your life? You can start that process right now by asking Jesus, the Jewish Messiah who is the heart of God's everlasting covenant, to come into your heart. Tell Him you want to accept His atoning sacrifice for your sins and that you want to accept His covenant and have an eternal loving relationship with Him.

FREE Lessons at www.BibleStudies.com

Call:
1-888-456-7933

Write:
Discover
P.O. Box 999
Loveland, CO 80539-099

It's easy to learn more about the Bible!